Egypt

a Lonely Planet travel atlas

Egypt – travel atlas

1st edition

Published by
Lonely Planet Publications
Head Office: PO Box 617, Hawthorn, Vic 3122, Australia
Branches: 155 Filbert St, Suite 251, Oakland, CA 94607, USA
          10 Barley Mow Passage, Chiswick, London W4 4PH, UK
          71 bis rue du Cardinal Lemoine, 75005 Paris, France

Cartography
Steinhart Katzir Publishers Ltd
Fax: 972-3-696-1360
email: 100264.721@compuserve.com

Printed by
Colorcraft Ltd, Hong Kong

Photographs
Glenn Beanland, Kristie Burns, Bethune Carmichael, Geert Cole, Greg Elms,
Leanne Logan, Tony Wheeler

Front Cover: Pyramids at sunrise, Giza (Kristie Burns)
Back Cover: Luxor Temple (Greg Elms)
Title page: Minarets at sunset, Hurghada (Leanne Logan)
Contents page: The Sphinx and the Pyramid of Chephren, Giza (Bethune Carmichael)

First Published
November 1996

**Although the authors and publisher have tried to make the information as accurate
as possible, they accept no responsibility for any loss, injury or inconvenience
sustained by any person using this book.**

National Library of Australia Cataloguing in Publication Data

Logan, Leanne & Cole, Geert
Egypt travel atlas

1st ed.
Includes index.
ISBN 0 86442 376 4

1. Egypt - Maps, Tourist.
2. Egypt - Road maps.
I. Logan, Leanne. II. Cole, Geert. (Series : Lonely Planet travel atlas).

912.62

Contents

Geert Cole and Leanne Logan

Born in Antwerp, Belgium, Geert swapped university and art studies in the 1970s to discover broader horizons and other cultures. Later, when not running his stained-glass studio, Geert could be found sailing the Pacific, sorting Aussie sheep, and amongst other challenges, trekking through Alaska and diving tropical reefs.

After completing a journalism degree, Leanne explored parts of her homeland as a reporter for Australian Associated Press before setting off through Asia and the Middle East to Europe and, eventually, Africa. Leanne joined Lonely Planet in 1991 and, while conducting research into Belgium's 350-odd beers, she met Geert, a local connoisseur.

The pair have been a team ever since, working on many Lonely Planet guides including *France, New Caledonia, Western Europe, India, Africa*, the *Middle East* and, most recently, *Egypt*. Researching the *Egypt travel atlas* took them from sand-blown oases to wind-swept beaches, and from the crowded streets of Cairo to ruined villages along the Nile.

Together they continue fossicking around this lovely planet.

About this Atlas

This book is another addition to the Lonely Planet travel atlas series. Designed to tie in with the equivalent Lonely Planet guidebook, we hope that the *Egypt travel atlas* will help travellers enjoy their trip even more. As well as detailed, accurate maps, this atlas also contains a multilingual map legend, useful travel information in five languages and a comprehensive index to ensure easy location-finding.

The maps were checked on the road by Leanne Logan and Geert Cole as part of their preparation for a new edition of Lonely Planet's *Egypt* guidebook.

From the Publishers

Thanks to Danny Schapiro, chief cartographer at Steinhart Katzir Publishers, who supervised production of this atlas. Danna Sharoni & Iris Sardes were responsible for the cartography. Iris also prepared the index. At Lonely Planet, editorial checking of the maps and index was completed by Lou Byrnes. Sally Jacka was responsible for the cartographic checking, design and layout of the atlas. David Kemp was responsible for cover design. Louise Klep finalised the layout and the cover. Paul Smitz edited the getting around section.

Lou Byrnes coordinated the translations. Thanks to translators Yoshiharu Abe, Christa Bouga-Hochstöger, Adrienne Costanzo, Pedro Diaz, Isabelle Muller, Caroline Guilleminot, Penelope Richardson & Sergio Mariscal. Special thanks to Rachel Scully and Geoff Stringer for their help in our hour of need.

Request

This atlas is designed to be clear, comprehensive and reliable. We hope you'll find it a worthy addition to your Lonely Planet travel library. Even if you don't, please let us know! We'd appreciate any suggestions you may have to make this product even better. Please complete and send us the feedback page at the back of this atlas to let us know exactly what you think.

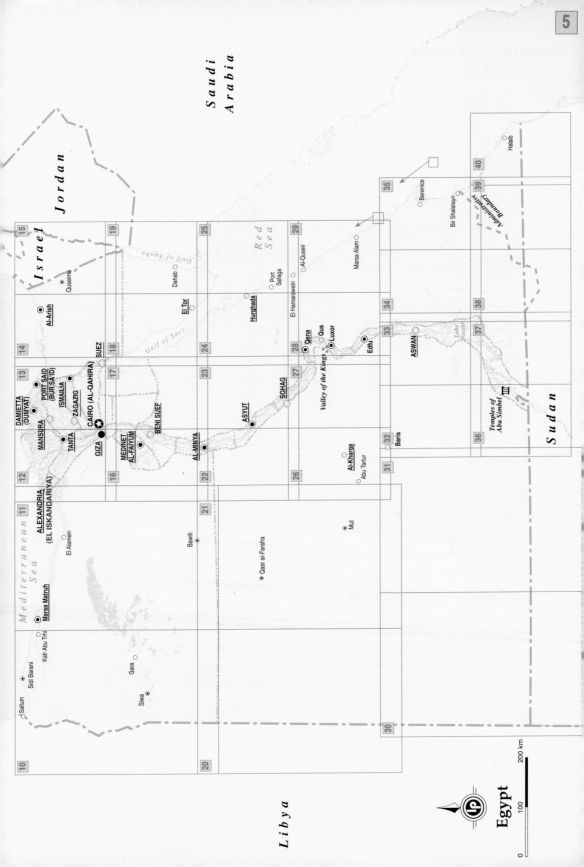

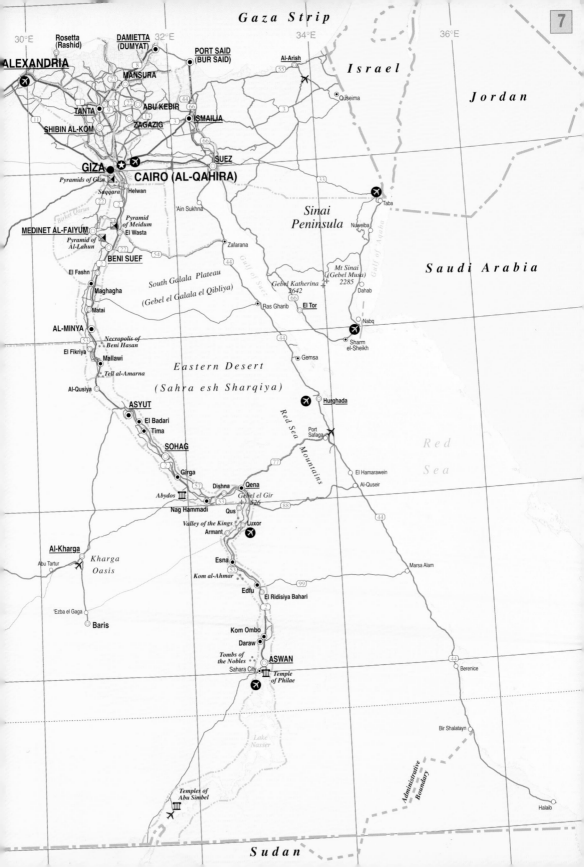

MAP LEGEND

Number of Inhabitants:

ALEXANDRIA > 2,500,000

GIZA ● 500,000 - 2,500,000

ISMAILIA ◉ 250,000 - 500,000

PORT SAID ◎ 100,000 - 250,000

Kafr El Dauwar ◉ 50,000 - 100,000

Abu Hummus ◎ 25,000 - 50,000

El Deir ◉ 10,000 -25,000

Baleqtar ○ <10,000

CAIRO Capital City
Capitale
Hauptstadt
Capital
首都

★ Capital City (Locator map)
Capitale (Carte de situation)
Hauptstadt (Orientierungskarte)
Capital (Mapa Localizador)
首都（地図上の位置）

<u>SUEZ</u> Governorate Capital
Capitale de gouvernorat
Regierungsbezirks Hauptstadt
Capital de la gobernación
行政区域の中心地

International Boundary
Limites Internationales
Staatsgrenze
Frontera Internacional
国境

Disputed Boundary
Frontière Contestée
umstrittene Grenze
Frontera Disputada
国境紛争境界線

Governorate Boundary
Limite de gouvernorat
Grenze des Regierungsbezirks
Límite de la gobernación
行政区域の境界線

Major Highway
Route Nationale
Femstraße
Carreterà Principal
主要な国道

Highway
Route Principale
Landstraße
Carretera
国道

Regional Road
Route Régionale
Regionale Fernstraße
Carretera Regional
地方道

Secondary Road
Route Secondaire
Nebenstraße
Carretera Secundaria
二級道路

Unsealed Road
Route non bitumée/piste
Unbefestigte Straße
Carretera sin Asfaltar
未舗装の道

Railway
Voie de chemin de fer
Eisenbahn
Ferrocarril
鉄道

El Mazar
Railway station
Gare Ferroviaire
Bahnhof
Estación de Ferrocarril
駅

55
Route Number
Numérotation Routière
Routenummer
Ruta Número
道路の番号

99
Distance in Kilometres
Distance en Kilomètres
Entfernung in Kilometern
Distancia en Kilómetros
距離（km）

Ferry Route
Route de ferry
Fährroute
Transbordador
フェリーの航路

✈ International Airport
Aéroport International
Internationaler Flughafen
Aeropuerto Internacional
国際空港

✈ Domestic Airport
　Aéroport National
　Inlandflughafen
　Aeropuerto Interior
　国内線空港

☀ Viewpoint
　Point de Vue
　Aussicht
　Mirador
　展望地点

Swamp
　Marais
　Sumpf
　Pantano
　沼地

⛩ Mosque
　Mosquée
　Moschee
　Mezquita
　モスク

Gebel Musa
2285 + Mountain
　Montagne
　Berg
　Montaña
　山

Desert
　Désert
　Wüste
　Desierto
　砂漠

† Church
　Église
　Kirche
　Iglesia
　教会

)(Pass
　Col
　Paß
　Desfiladero
　峠

Reef
　Falaise
　Riff
　Arrecife
　岩礁

⊠ Pyramid
　Pyramide
　Pyramide
　Pirámide
　ピラミッド

National Park
　Parc National
　Nationalpark
　Parque Nacional
　国立公園

.... Tropics
　Tropiques
　Tropen
　Los Trópicos
　回帰線

🏛 Temple
　Temple
　Tempel
　Templo
　寺院

◓ Cave
　Grotte
　Höhle
　Cueva
　洞窟

⬛ Tomb
　Tombeau
　Grab
　Tumba
　墓

～ River
　Fleuve/Rivière
　Fluß
　Río
　川

∴ Ruins
　Ruines
　Ruinen
　Ruinas
　遺跡

～ Wadi
　Wadi
　Wadi
　Uadi
　ワジ

3000 m
2500 m
2100 m
1800 m
1500 m
1200 m
900 m
600 m
300 m
0
-300

🗼 Lighthouse
　Phare
　Leuchtturm
　Faro
　灯台

◯ Lake
　Lac
　See
　Lago
　湖

⛴ Seaport
　Port de Mer
　Seehafen
　Puerto Marítimo
　港

🌴 Oasis
　Oasis
　Oase
　Oasis
　オアシス

0　10　20　30　40km

Eastern Egypt 1 : 900 000

⚓ Shipwreck
　Épave
　Schiffbruch
　Naufragio
　難破船

⚬～ Spring/Well
　Source/Puits
　Quelle/Brunnen
　Manantial/Pozo
　泉／井戸

0　20　40　60　80km

Western Egypt 1 : 1 800 000

▲ Camping Ground
　Terrain de Camping
　Zeltplatz
　Camping
　キャンプ場

● Beach
　Plage
　Strand
　Playa
　海岸

Universal Transverse

Mercator projection

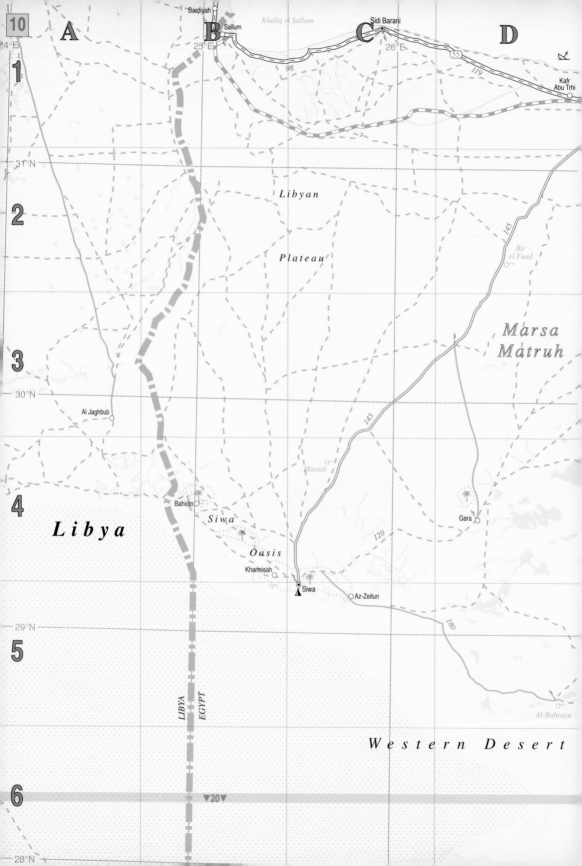

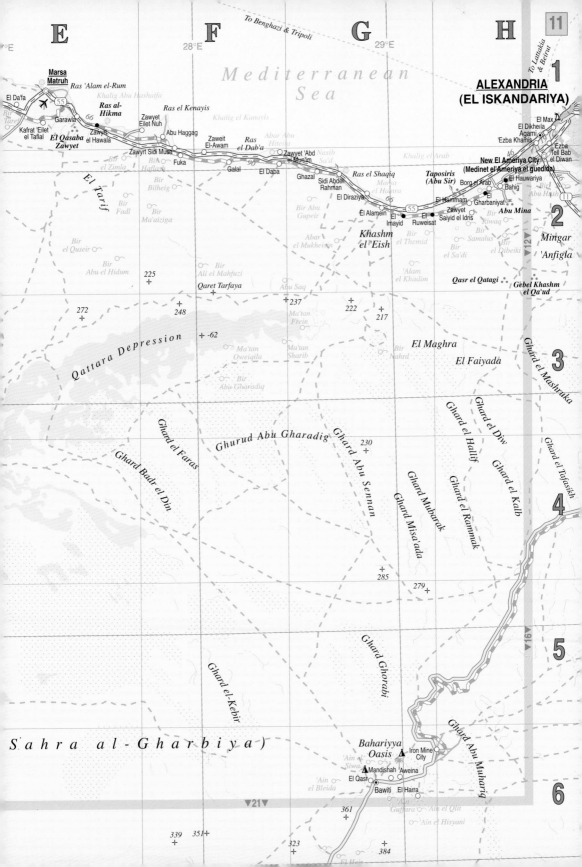

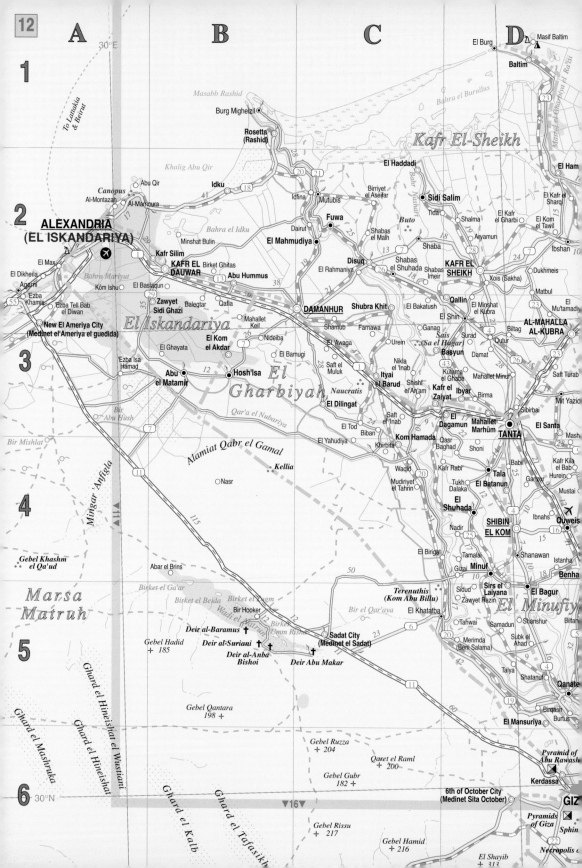

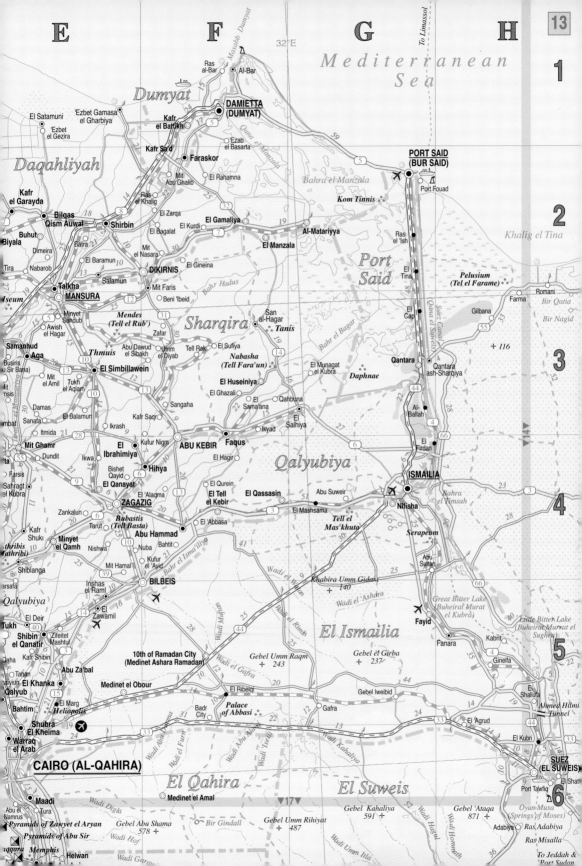

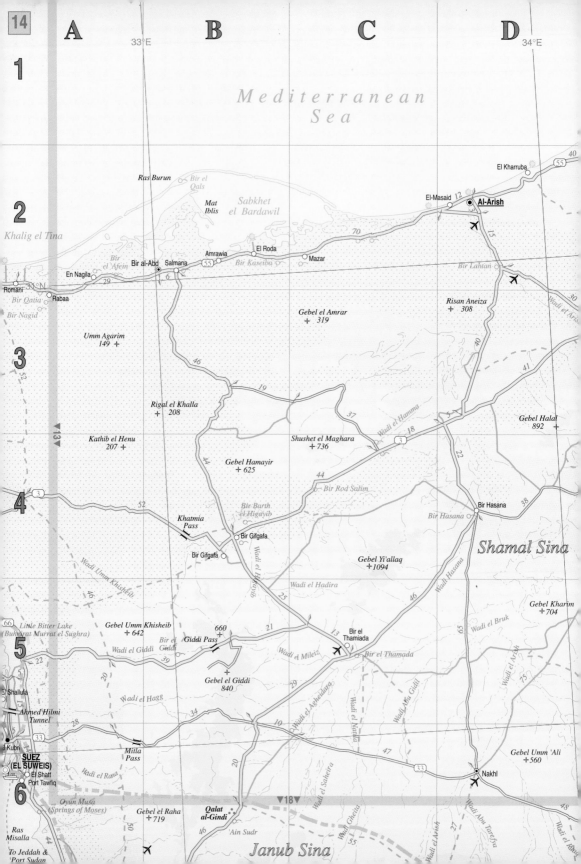

14

A   B   C   D

33°E   34°E

1

M e d i t e r r a n e a n
S e a

2

El Kharruba

40
55

Ras Burun
Bir el Qals

El-Masaid 12 ● **Al-Arish**

Mat Iblis
Sabkhet el Bardawil

15

Khalig el Tina

70

Amrawia El Roda

Bir el Afein
Bir al-Abd Salmana
En Nagila 55
Romani 29 6
Bir Qatia Rabaa
Bir Nagid

Mazar

Bir Kaseiba

Bir Lahfan

30
Wadi el Arish

3

Gebel el Amrar
+ 319

Risan Aneiza
+ 308

Umm Agarim
149 +

46

19

40

41

Rigal el Khalla
+ 208

Wadi el Hamma

Gebel Halal
892 +

Kathib el Henu
207 +

Shushet el Maghara
+ 736

18
3

37

44

Gebel Hamayir
+ 625

44

22

▼13▼
52

4

3

52

Khatmia Pass

Bir Barth el Higayib

Bir Rod Salim

Bir Hasana

38

Bir Hasana

Shamal Sina

Bir Gifgafa

Bir Gifgafa

Gebel Yi'allaq
+1094

Wadi Hasana

Wadi el Hadira

46

65

Wadi el Bruk

Gebel Kharim
+704

66
Little Bitter Lake
(Buheyrat Murrat el Sughra)

Gebel Umm Khisheib
+ 642

Wadi Umm Khisheib

46

Wadi el Giddi

Bir el Giddi
Giddi Pass

660
+

25

21

Wadi el Miletz

13
Bir el Thamiada

Bir el Thamada

Wadi Abu Gidil

Wadi el Arish

5

5

22

20

39

Gebel el Giddi
840

+

29

Wadi el Hagg

34

10

Wadi el Agheidera

Wadi el Natila

75

El Shallufa

Ahmed Hilmi Tunnel

28

Milla Pass

20

47

Gebel Umm 'Ali
+ 560

33
El Kubri
33

Wadi el Rana

SUEZ (EL SUWEIS) El Shatt
Port Tawfiq

Oyun Musa (Springs of Moses)

Gebel el Raha
+ 719

Qalat al-Gindi

'Ain Sudr

Wadi el Saheira

Wadi Gheita

27

Wadi Abu Tarefha

48

Wadi el Arish

33
Nakhl

6

Ras Misalla

To Jeddah & Port Sudan

44

50

46

▼18▼

20

55

Janub Sina

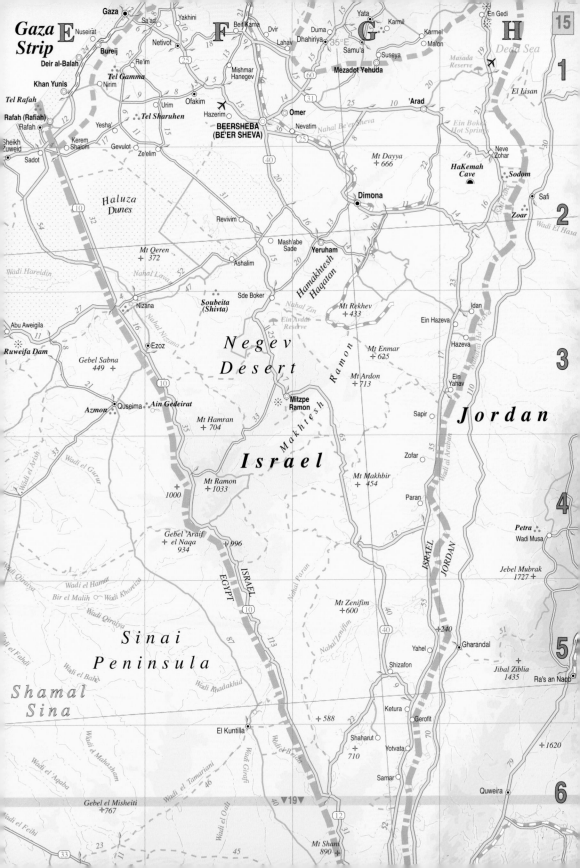

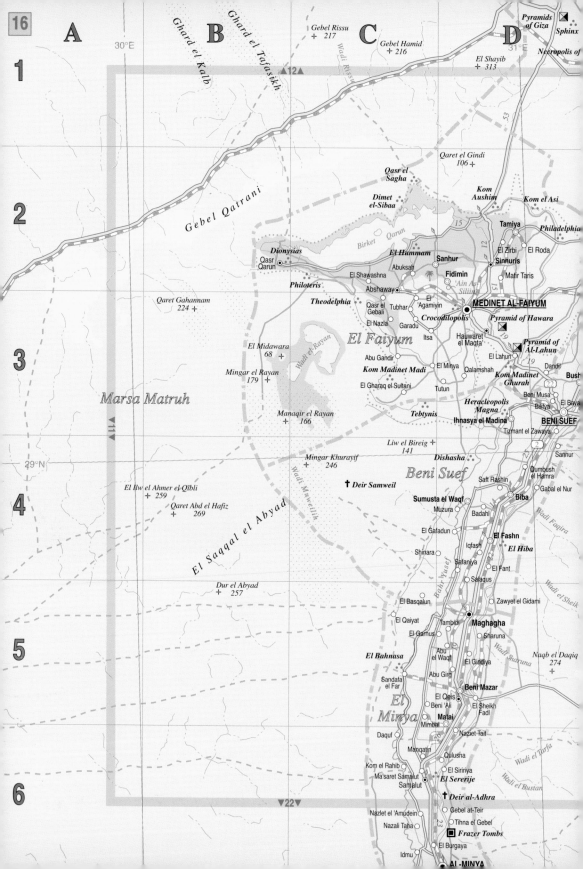

A   B   C   D

1

2

3

4

5

6

Pyramids
of Giza

Sphinx

Necropolis of

Ghard el Kalb

Ghard el Tafasikh

Gebel Rissu
+ 217

Gebel Hamid
+ 216

El Shayib
+ 313

Wadi Rissu

30°E

31°E

53

▲12▲

Qaret el Gindi
106 +

Gebel Qatrani

Qasr el
Sagha

Dimet
el-Sibaa

Kom
Aushim

Kom el Asi

Birket Qarun

15

Tamiya

Philadelphia

12

El Zirbi

El Roda

Dionysias

Qasr
Qarun

El Hammam

Sanhur

Sinnuris

Mafir Taris

15

Abuksah

Philoteris

El Shawashna

Fidimin

Qaret Gahannam
224 +

Theodelphia

Abshaway

El
'Agamiyin

'Ain Asl
Silin

MEDINET AL-FAIYUM

Qasr el
Gebali

Tubhar

Crocodilopolis

Pyramid of Hawara

El Nazla

Garadu

Hauwaret
el Maqta

19

Pyramid of
Al-Lahun

El Midawara
68 +

Wadi el Rayan

El Faiyum

Itsa

El Lahun

19

Dandil

Mingar el Rayan
179 +

Abu Gandir

El Minya

Qalamshah

Kom Madinet
Ghurah

Bush

Marsa Matruh

Kom Madinet Madi

El Gharaq el Sultani

Tutun

Beni Musa
Bilitya

22

El Bawa

Manaqir el Rayan
166 +

Tebtynis

Heracleopolis
Magna

Ihnasya el Madina

BENI SUEF

2

29°N

Liw el Bireig
141 +

Tizmant el Zawaya

Sannur

▼11▼

Mingar Khurayif
246 +

Dishasha

Beni Suef

Saft Rashin

Qumbush
el Hamra

El Ilw el Ahmer el Qibli
+ 259

✝ Deir Samweil

Sumusta el Waqf

Muzura

Badahl

Gabal el Nur

Biba

Qaret Abd el Hafiz
+ 269

Wadi Muweilih

El Saqqal el Abyad

El Gafadun

Iqfash

El Fashn

Wadi Faqira

Shinara

Safaniya

El Hiba

El Fant

Dur el Abyad
+ 257

Salaqus

Bahr Yusef

El Basqalun

Zawyet el Gidami

Wadi el Sheik

El Qaiyat

Tambidi

Maghagha

El Garnus

Sharuna

Wadi Sharuna

Naqb el Daqiq
274 +

El Bahnasa

Abu
el Waqi

El Gindiya

Abu Girg

Sandafa
el Far

Beni Mazar

El Minya

El Qeis

Beni 'Ali

El Sheikh
Fadl

Matai

Mimbal

Naziet Tait

Daquf

Manqatin

Qulusna

Kom el Rahib

El Siririya

Ma'saret Samalut

El Sererije

Samalut

✝ Deir al-Adhra

Nazlet el 'Amudein

Gebel at-Teir

Nazali Tana

Tihna el Gebel

■ Frazer Tombs

Idmu

El Burgaya

▼22▼

AL-MINYA

Pyramids of Zawyet el Aryan
Tura
Pyramids of Abu Sir
Saqqara Memphis
Helwan
Saqqara
Al-Badrashein
Dahshur
Pyramids of Dahshur
El Tabbin
El Minya
15th of May City
(Medineth 15 Mayo)
El Iknsas el Qibliya
Harnasht
El 'Att
El Hai
El 'Aiyat
Bamha
El Fahmiyim
El Saff
Maharrada
El Widy
El Qubabat
Pyramid Meidum
Meidum
El Wasta
El Burumbul
El Ma'mun
'shmant
El Shanawiya

E

Gebel Abu Shama
578 +
Bir Gindall

Wadi Hof
Wadi Garawi

Sheikh
Salama

Bir el
'Agramiya

Wadi Hayira

El Giza

Bir
Afandina

Wadi el Wirag

Wadi el Nu'umiya

Wadi Atfih

Wadi Lishyab

Wadi Rishrash

F

Gebel Umm Rihiyat
+ 487

Wadi Umm Itla

▲13▲

Wadi Gharba

Wadi el Shuna

Naqb Ghul
861 +

Wadi Qena

Kulet el Qrein
+ 897

G

Gebel Kahaliya
591 +

Gebel Akheidir
367 +

Wadi Hugul

El Suweis

North Galala Plateau
(Gebel el Galala el Bahariya)

Wadi Ghuweibba

'Ain Sukhna

Wadi No'oz

Wadi Abyad

H

Gebel 'Ataqa
871 +

Ras
Adabiya
Adabiya

Ras
Misalla

Gulf
of
Suez

Bir
Udeit

Bir
Bad

Wadi Hommath

Wadi Rad

Ghubbet
el Bus

Suez-Jeddah-Port Sudan

Ras Abu
Darag

70

17

1

2

3

Wadi Samnur

Wadi 'Abu Risha

54 82

Wadi Arhab

Wadi Sanur

Wadi Muathil

Bir
el Ghamir

Wadi Abu Rimth

Wadi el Nihaya

Wadi Abu Kharaga

Gineinet el Atash
318 +

Wadi Quss

Wadi 'Irkas

Wadi Askhar

El Tileimat
223 +

89

Wadi 'Araba

Bir
Buerat

Monastery of St Anthony
(Deir el Qaddis Antwian)

Gebel Thilmet +
656

Monastery of St Paul
(Deir Mari Bolos)

18

4

Wadi el 'Abeid

South Galala Plateau
(Gebel el Galala el Qibliya)

1464 +

1206 +

Bir el
Dakhal

Wadi Umm Aria

5 +

Al-Bahr
al-Ahmar

Gebel Umm Tinassib
1110

Bir
Mureir

Khasm el Raqaba
483 +

253

Wadi el Tarfa

Wadi Tarfa

Wadi Hawashiya

Gebel Samr el Qa
893 +

6

▼23▼

Eastern Desert
(Sahra ash-Sharqiya)

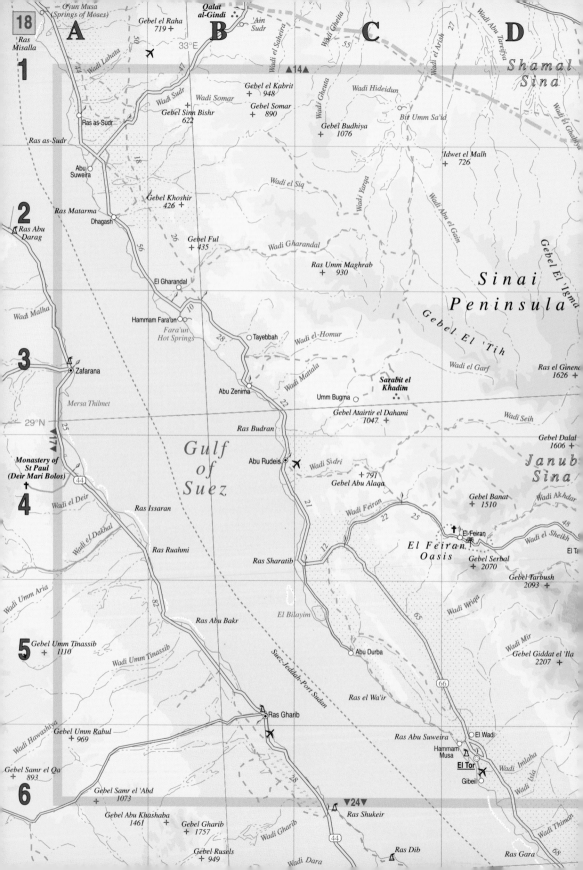

A   **B**   **C**   **D**

Oyun Musa
(Springs of Moses)

Qalat al-Gindi

'Ain Sudr

Wadi el Sobeira

Wadi Gheita

Wadi Abu Tarefja

Ras Misalla

Gebel el Raha
719 +

33°E

Shamal Sina

1

▲14▲

Wadi Lahata

50

41

Wadi el Arish

27

Wadi el Ghabia

Gebel el Kabrit
+ 948

Wadi Hideidun

Wadi Sudr

Wadi Somar

Gebel Somar
+ 890

Gebel Sinn Bishr
622

Ras as-Sudr

18

Gebel Budhiya
+ 1076

Bir Umm Sa'id

Ras as-Sudr

Abu Suweira

'Idwet el Malh
726

2

Ras Abu Darag

Ras Matarma

Gebel Khoshir
426 +

Wadi el Siq

Wadi Abu el Gain

Wadi Yarga

Sinai Peninsula

Gebel El 'Igma

Dhagash

56

26

Gebel Ful
+ 435

Wadi Gharandal

Ras Umm Maghrab
+ 930

Gebel El 'Tih

El Gharandal

10

Wadi Malha

Hammam Fara'un
*Fara'un
Hot Springs*

28

Tayebbah

Wadi el-Homur

Wadi el Garf

Ras el Ginena
1626 +

3

Zafarana

Abu Zenima

22

Wadi Mattala

Umm Bugma

Sarabit el Khadim

Wadi Seih

29°N

Mersa Thilmet

25

Ras Budran

Gebel Atairtir el Dahami
1047 +

Gebel Dalal
1606 +

Janub Sina

Monastery of St Paul
(Deir Mari Bolos)

▼17▼

*Gulf
of
Suez*

Abu Rudeis

Wadi Sidri

+ 791
Gebel Abu Alaqa

Gebel Banat
+ 1510

Wadi Akhdar

4

44

Wadi el Deir

Ras Issaran

21

Wadi Feiran

22

25

El-Feiran

Wadi el Sheikh

48

Wadi el Dakhal

Ras Ruahmi

12

*El Feiran
Oasis*

Gebel Serbal
+ 2070

El Ta

Ras Sharatib

Gebel Tarbush
2093 +

Wadi Umm Aria

El Bilayim

82

Wadi Wiaa

65

5

Gebel Umm Tinassib
+ 1110

Ras Abu Bakr

Wadi Mir

Gebel Giddat el 'Ila
2207 +

Wadi Umm Tinassib

Abu Durba

Ras el Wa'ir

66

Suez–Jeddah–Port Sudan

Ras Abu Suweira

El Wadi

Gebel Umm Rabul
+ 969

Wadi Hawashiya

Ras Gharib

Hammam Musa

El Tor

Wadi Imtaha

Gebel Samr el Qa
+ 893

28

Gibeil

Wadi Isla

6

Gebel Samr el 'Abd
1073

44

▼24▼

Ras Shukeir

Wadi Thiman

Gebel Abu Khashaba
1461 +

Gebel Gharib
+ 1757

Wadi Gharib

Wadi Dara

Ras Dib

Ras Gara

68

Gebel Rusels
+ 949

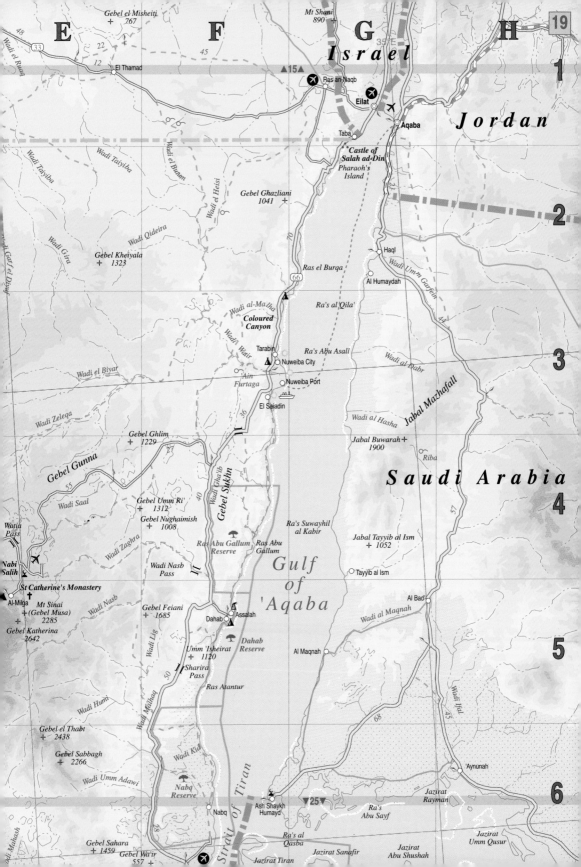

E   **F**   **G**   **H**

Gebel el Misheiti
+ 767

Mt Shani
890 ▲

Wadi el Ruaq

33

48

22

45

12

El Thamad

▲15▲

Ras an-Naqb

Israel

1

Wadi Taiyiba

Wadi el Biaan

Wadi el Heisi

Eilat

Aqaba

Jordan

Taba

Wadi Taiyiba

35°E

Castle of
Salah ad-Din

Pharaoh's
Island

Gebel Ghazliani
1041 +

Wadi Qideira

Wadi Gira

70

Ras el Burqa

Haql

Al Humaydah

Wadi Umm Garfein

2

Gebel Kheiyala
+ 1323

66

Ra's al 'Qila'

36°E

44

Gebel Douf el

Wadi al-Malha

Wadi Watir

*Coloured
Canyon*

Tarabin

Ra's Abu Asall

Wadi al Dabr

Jabal Mazhafall

3

Wadi el Biyar

Ain
Furtaga

Nuweiba City

Nuweiba Port

El Saiadin

Wadi al Hasha

Wadi Zeleqa

Gebel Ghlim
+ 1229

36

Jabal Buwarah +
1900

Riba

Gebel Gunna

55

27

Gebel Umm Ri'
+ 1312

Gebel Nughaimish
+ 1008

40

Wadi Gha'ib

Gebel Sukhn

Ra's Suwayhil
al Kabir

Saudi Arabia

4

Wadi Saal

Wadi Zaghra

Ras Abu Gallum
Reserve

Ras Abu
Gallum

Jabal Tayyib al Ism
+ 1052

57

Watia
Pass

**Nabi
Salih**

Wadi Nasb
Pass

**Gulf
of
'Aqaba**

Tayyib al Ism

St Catherine's Monastery

Al-Milga

Mt Sinai
+ (Gebel Musa)
2285

Wadi Nasb

Gebel Feiani
+ 1685

Dahab

Assalah

Al Bad

5

Gebel Katherina
2642

Wadi Lib

Wadi al Maqnah

Umm 'Isheirat
+ 1120

50

*Dahab
Reserve*

Al Maqnah

Sharira
Pass

Ras Atantur

Wadi Mathaq

Wadi Hal

68

45

Gebel el Thabt
+ 2438

Gebel Sabbagh
+ 2266

Wadi Kid

*Nabq
Reserve*

'Aynunah

Jazirat
Rayman

6

Wadi Umm Adawi

Wadi Humr

*Nabq
Reserve*

Nabq

Ash Shaykh
Humayd

▼25▼

Ra's
Abu Sayf

Jazirat
Abu Shushah

Jazirat
Umm Qusur

Gebel Sahara
+ 1459

Gebel Wa'ir
+ 557

28

Strait of Tiran

Ra's al
Qasba

Jazirat Sanafir

Jazirat Tiran

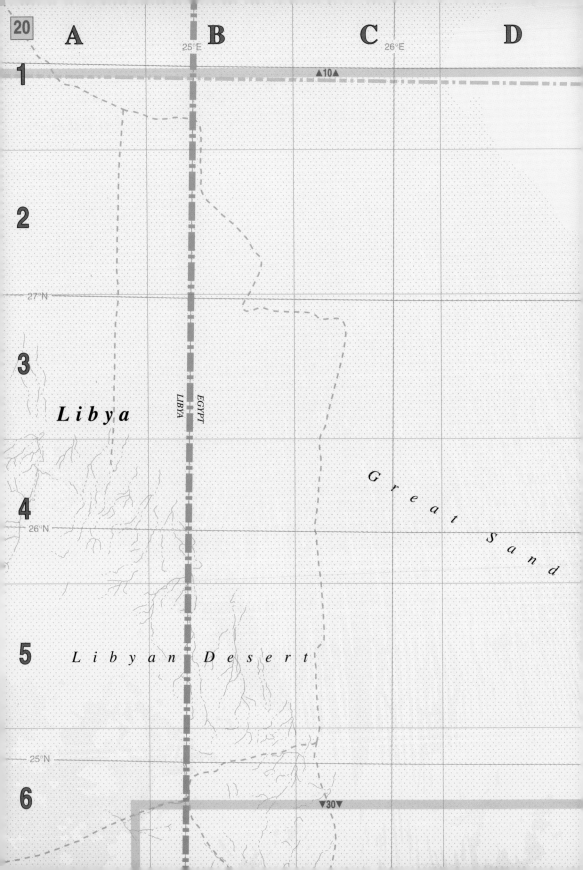

A   B   C   D

25°E

26°E

1

▲10▲

2

27°N

3

LIBYA   EGYPT

Libya

G r e a t   S a n d

4

26°N

5

L i b y a n   D e s e r t

25°N

6

▼30▼

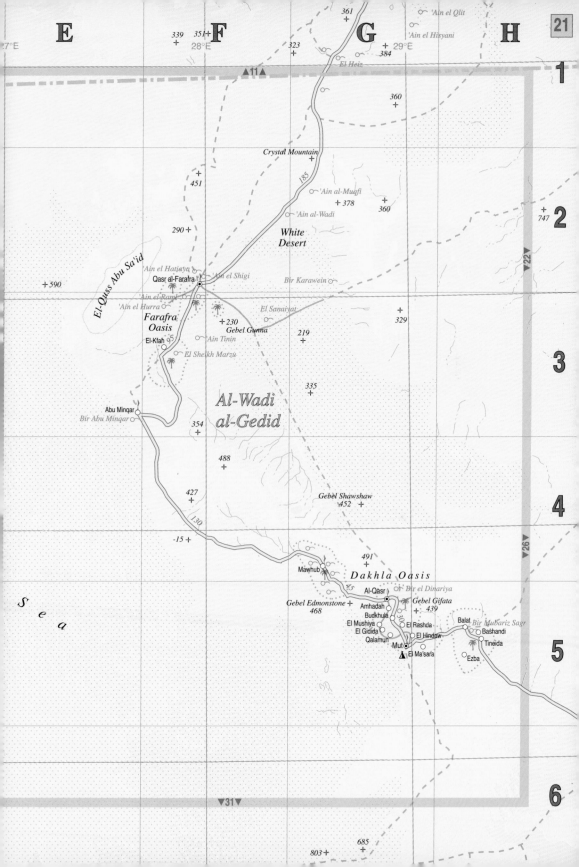

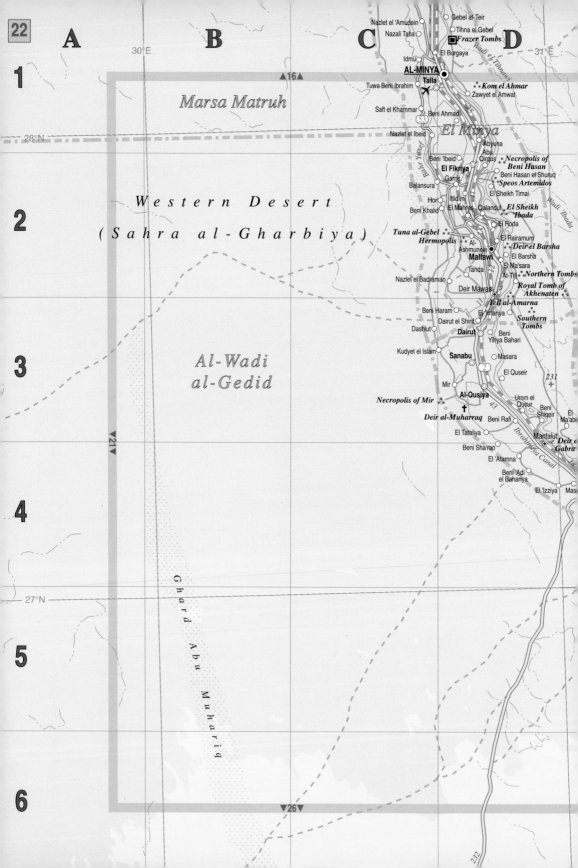

A   **B**   **C**   **D**

30°E

31°E

1

▲16▲

Marsa Matruh

28°N

El Minya

2

W e s t e r n   D e s e r t

(S a h r a   a l - G h a r b i y a)

3

Al-Wadi

al-Gedid

◄21▼

4

27°N

5

G h a r d   A b u   M u h a r r i q

6

▼26▼

Nazlet el 'Amudein
Nazali Taha
Idmu
El Burgaya
AL-MINYA
Talla
Tuwa Beni Ibrahim
Saft el Khammar
Beni Ahmad
53
Nazlet el Ibeid
Abyuha
Abu
Beni 'Ibeid
Qirqus
El Fikriya
Garris
Balansura
Hor
Beni Khalid
Itlidim
El Mahras
Qalandul
El Roda
Tuna al-Gebel
Hermopolis
Al-Ashmunein
Mallawi
Tanda
At-Till
Nazlet el Badraman
Deir Mawas
El Ihariya
Beni Haram
Dairut el Shirif
Dashlut
Dairut
Beni Yihya Bahari
Kudyet el Islam
Sanabu
Masara
2
Mir
El Quseir
231
Umm el
Qusur
Al-Qusiya
Necropolis of Mir
43
Beni
Shiqeir
Deir al-Muharraq
Beni Rafi
El Tataliya
Manfalut
Beni Sha'ran
El 'Atamna
Beni 'Adi
el Bahariya
El 'Izziya

Gebel at-Teir
Tihna el Gebel
Frazer Tombs
Kom el Ahmar
Zawyet el Amwat
Necropolis of
Beni Hasan
Beni Hasan el Shuruq
Speos Artemidos
El Sheikh Timai
El Sheikh
Ibada
El Rairamum
Deir el Barsha
El Barsha
El Ma'sara
Northern Tombs
Royal Tomb of
Akhenaten
Tell al-Amarna
Southern
Tombs

Bahr Yusef

Wadi el Tihnawi

Wadi 'Ibada

Ibrahimiya Canal

Deir el
Gabra

232

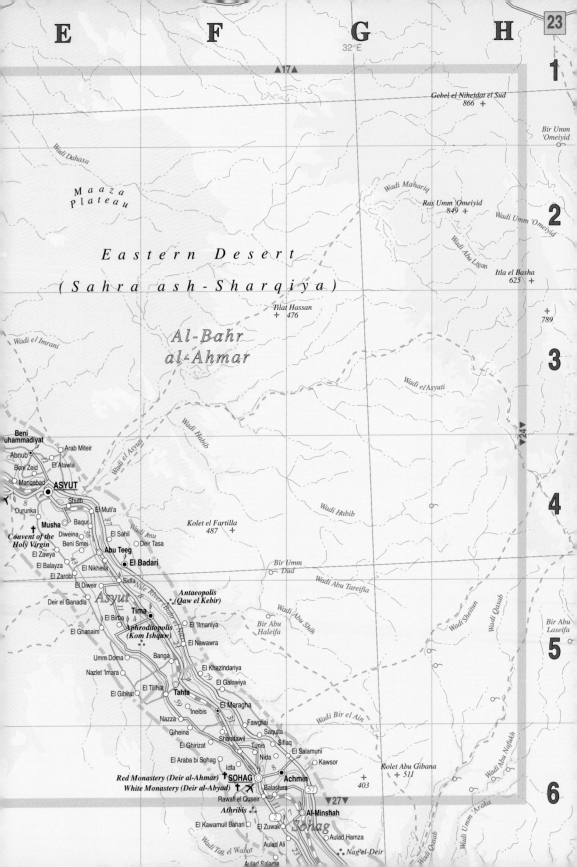

32°E

▲17▲

Gebel el Niheidat el Sud
866 +

Bir Umm
'Omeiyid

Wadi Dahasa

M a a z a
P l a t e a u

Wadi Mahariq

Ras Umm 'Omeiyid
849 +

Wadi Umm 'Omeiyid

Wadi Abu Ligan

Itla el Basha
625 +

E a s t e r n   D e s e r t

(S a h r a   a s h - S h a r q i y a)

Tilat Hassan
+ 476

+
789

Al-Bahr
al-Ahmar

Wadi el Imrani

Wadi el Asyuti

▼24▼

Wadi Habib

Beni
uhammadiyat

Arab Miteir

Abnub

Beni Zeid

El Atawla

Mariqabad

ASYUT

Shutb

Wadi Asyut

Durunka

El Muti'a

Kolet el Fartilla
487 +

Wadi Habib

Musha

Baqur

Diweina

El Sahil

Convent of the
Holy Virgin

Beni Smei

Deir Tasa

El Zawya

Abu Teeg

El Balayza

El Nikheila

● **El Badari**

Bir Umm
Dud

El Zarobl

Sidfa

Wadi Abu Tareifia

El Diweir

Deir el Ganadla

Asyut

Antaeopolis
(Qaw el Kebir)

El Ghanaim

El Birba

Tima

Wadi Abu Shih

El 'Itmaniya

Bir Abu
Haleifa

Wadi Shutun

Wadi Qasab

Bir Abu
Laseifa

Aphroditopolis
(Kom Ishqaw)

El Nawawra

Umm Doma

Banga

Nazlet 'Imara

El Khazindariya

El Galawiya

El Gibirat

El Tilihat

Tahta

El Maragha

Wadi Abu Nidfukh

'Ineibis

Nazza

Fawgilai

Saquita

Wadi Bir el Ain

Giheina

Shandawil

Tunis

Siflaq

El Ghirizat

Nida

El Salamuni

El Araba bi Sohag

Idfa

Kawsor

Kolet Abu Gibana
+ 511

Red Monastery (Deir al-Ahmar) ✝ **✝SOHAG** ✈
White Monastery (Deir al-Abyad) ✝

Achmin

+
403

Rawafi el Quseir

Balashura

▼27▼

Athribis

Al-Minshah

Sohag

Wadi Umm 'Araka

El Kawamuil Bahari

El Zuwak

Aulad Hamza

Wadi Tag el Wabar

Aulad Ali

Nag'el-Deir

Aulad Salama

Wadi Qasab

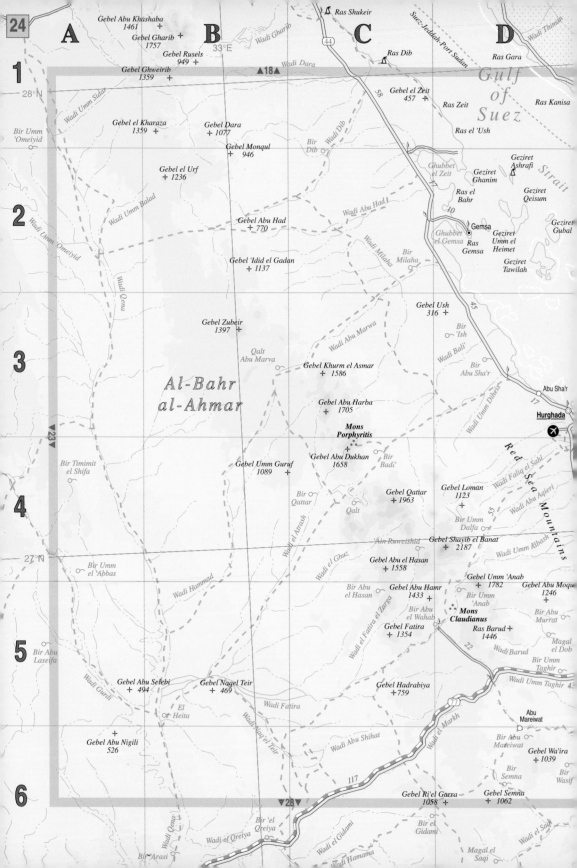

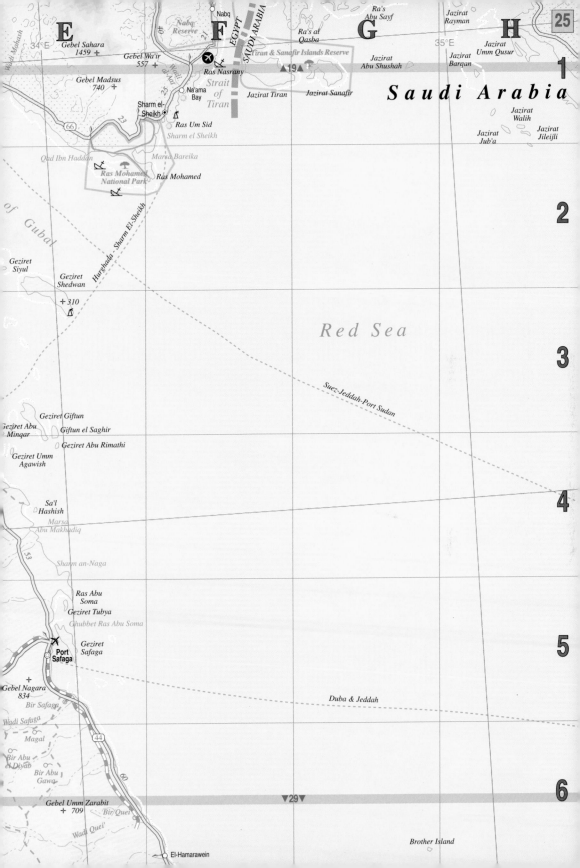

E   **F**   EGYPT   SAUDI ARABIA   **G**   **H**

Wadi Mahash   34°E

Nabq

Nabq Reserve

Ra's Abu Sayf   Jazirat Rayman

Jazirat Umm Qusur

Gebel Sahara 1459

Gebel Wa'ir 557

Ra's al Qasba

Tiran & Sanafir Islands Reserve

Jazirat Abu Shushah

35°E   Jazirat Barqan

Wadi al-Aat

▲19▲

1

Gebel Madsus 740

Na'ama Bay

Strait of Tiran

Jazirat Tiran   Jazirat Sanafir

S a u d i   A r a b i a

Sharm el-Sheikh

Ras Um Sid

Sharm el Sheikh

Jazirat Walih

Jazirat Jub'a   Jazirat Jileijli

Qad Ibn Haddan

Marsa Bareika

Ras Mohamed National Park   Ras Mohamed

2

of Gubal

Geziret Siyul

Geziret Shedwan

Hurghada - Sharm El Sheikh

+310

R e d   S e a

3

Suez-Jeddah-Port Sudan

Geziret Giftun

Geziret Abu Minqar

Giftun el Saghir

Geziret Abu Rimathi

Geziret Umm Agawish

Sa'l Hashish

Marsa Abu Makhadiq

4

53

Sharm an-Naga

Ras Abu Soma

Geziret Tubya

Ghubbet Ras Abu Soma

Geziret Safaga

Port Safaga

Geziret Safaga

5

Gebel Nagara 834

Bir Safaga

Duba & Jeddah

Wadi Safaga

Magal

44

Bir Abu el Diyab

Bir Abu Gawa

60

6

Gebel Umm Zarabit 709   Bir Quei

▼29▼

Wadi Quei

El-Hamarawein

Brother Island

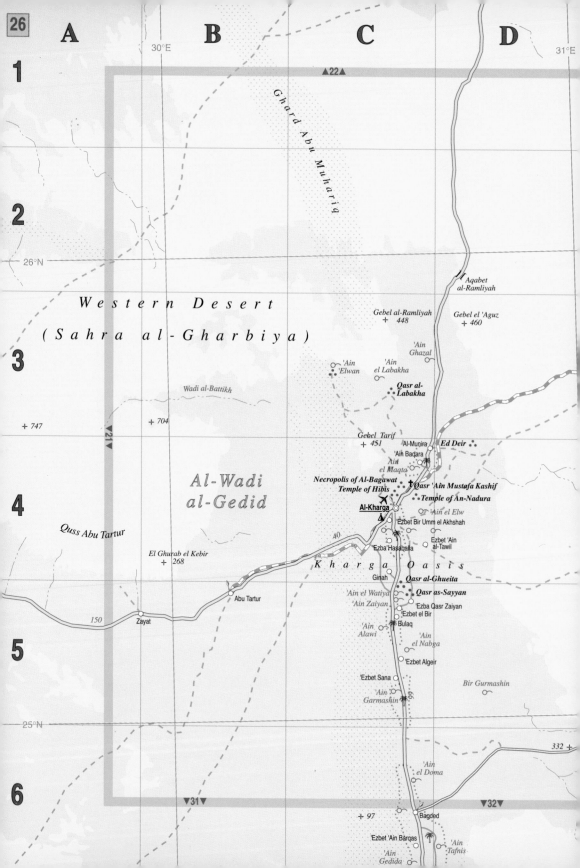

A   B   C   D

1

▲22▲

30°E   31°E

Ghard Abu Muhariq

2

26°N

W e s t e r n   D e s e r t

(S a h r a   a l - G h a r b i y a)

Aqabet
al-Ramliyah

Gebel al-Ramliyah
+ 448

Gebel el 'Aguz
+ 460

'Ain
Ghazal

3

'Ain
'Elwan

'Ain
el Labakha

**Qasr al-
Labakha**

Wadi al-Battikh

+ 747

+ 704

Gebel Tarif
+ 451   Al-Munira   **Ed Deir**

▼21▼

'Ain Baqara

'Ain
el Maqta

Necropolis of Al-Bagawat   **†** *Qasr 'Ain Mustafa Kashif*
Temple of Hibis

*Al-Wadi
al-Gedid*

• Temple of An-Nadura

Al-Kharga

4

'Ain el Elw

Quss Abu Tartur

A0

'Ezbet Bir Umm el Akhshah

Ezba Hasaballa

Ezbet 'Ain
al-Tawil

El Ghurab el Kebir
+ 268

K h a r g a   O a s i s

Qasr al-Ghueita

Ginah

'Ain el Watiya   **Qasr as-Sayyan**

Abu Tartur

'Ain Zaiyan

'Ezba Qasr Zaiyan

'Ezbet el Bir

150

Bulaq

Zayat

'Ain
Alawi

'Ain
el Nabga

5

Ezbet Algeir

'Ezbet Sana

Bir Gurmashin

'Ain
Garmashin

25°N

332 +

'Ain
el Doma

6

▼31▼

▼32▼

+ 97   Bagded

'Ezbet 'Ain Bärqas

'Ain
Tafnis

'Ain
Gedida

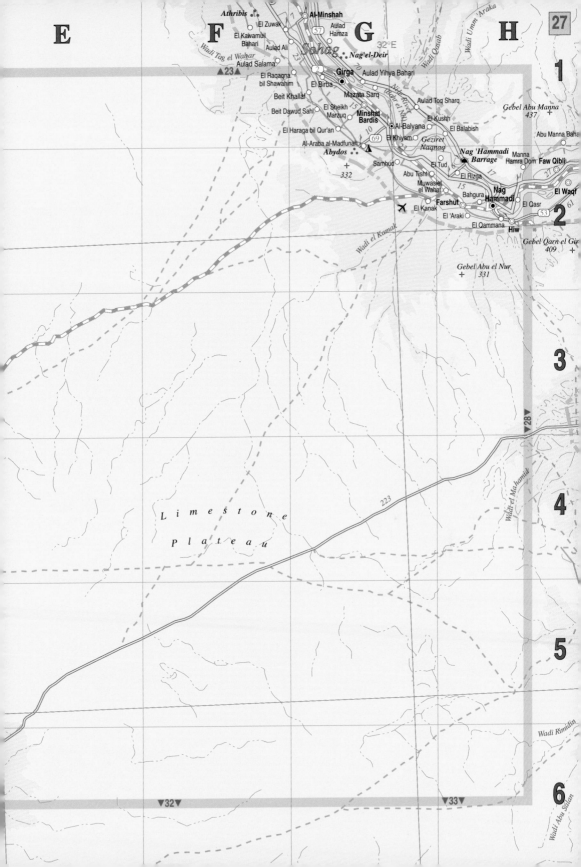

A B C D

1

Wadi el Miyat
Wadi Shahaden
Wadi Qena
Bir 'el Oreiya
Bir el Gidami
Magal el Saqi
33°E
Wadi el Oreiya
Wadi el Gidami
Bir 'Arasi
Wadi Hamama
▲24▲
Gebel el Sheikh Isa
439 +
Gebel Abu Manna
+ 437
El Ghawasa
El Makhadma
Gebel el Gir
+ 508
Bir el Gidami
Gebel el Rubshi
+ 996
Abu Manna Bahari
Abu Diyab
30
●**Qena**
El Gabalaw
Gebel el Surai
+ 657
Wadi el Atesni
Wadi Umm Had
Bir el Kubbaniya
Gebel Mi'tiq
1112
Faw Qibli
Dishna
Aulad
53
Dendara (Tantyra)
El Tiweirat
Gebel el Gir
+ 526
Abnud
Wadi el Surai
Bir 'Ambar
Wadi el Maweih el Atshan
Bir el Hammamat
107
Bir el Sid
Bir Umm Fawakhir
Et Re'ia

2

26°N
El Waqi
Gebel Sinn el Gir
+ 409
Qena
El Ballas
El Zawayda
Ombos
El Sheikhiya
El Barahma
Qift
El 'Ileiqat
88
Qasr el Banat
Gebel Shihimiya
659
Bir el Sid
Bir Nur
Naqada
Qus▲
Shanhul
2
Wadi el Mathula
Wadi Rod Ayid
Bir el Qash
Wadi el Qash
Danfiq
Garagus
Higaza
El Laqeita
Wadi el Qash

3

Deir Mari Buktur †
Deir el Melak †
El Qibli Qamula
El Zeiniya Qibli
Khuzam
25
Wadi Zaidun
Valley of the Kings ■
Valley of the Nobles ■
Temples of Karnak
Luxor
El Madamud
Wadi el Khuzam
Wadi Mishash
Wadi Manih
E a s t e r n   D e s e r t
Valley of the Queens ■
✈
El Bayadiya
El Metmar †
Armant
El Dab'iya
El Rizeiqat
El Rayayna
Tod
El Idisat
Gebel el Nezzi
670 +
Wadi el Madamul
Wadi Umm Theidha
Wadi el Shaghab
Wadi Uqdiya
(S a h r a   a s h - S h a r q i y a)
El Dimugrat
El Shaghab

4

Mo'alla
El Gabalein
El Mi'alla
Aphroditopolis
Gebel el Rakhamiya
+ 701
Gebel el Shalul
+ 697
Bir el Shalul
Kiman el Mata'na
53
Asfun el Mata'na
Mata'na
El Nugu
El Homra el Shanka
606 +
El Deir
Esna ●
El Hilla
Wadi el Shaki
Wadi Abu 'Igeidi
Temple of Khnum
El 'Adayma

5

El Siba'iya
Nag'el Ma'mariya
El Mahamid
Al-Kab (Nekheb)
Wadi el Barramiya
50
Wadi el Radda
Wadi Khebar
Wadi Iham
El Bisaliya Qibli
Kom al-Ahmar (Nekhen)
Kom el Ahmar
El Sa'ayda Qibli
El Kilh Sharq
El Kilh Gharb
58
Wadi 'Abbad
Bir 'Abbad
El Kanayis Temple
99
El Kanayis
Wadi el Miyah
25°N
Edfu ●
Temple of Horus
Aswan ◎
El Ridisiya Bahari
El Ridisiya Qibli
Gebel Serag
El Sirag
Wadi Sillim

6

Wadi Rimidan
Al-Wadi al-Gedid
Wadi Abu Salan
▼33▼
2
43
Wadi el Sirag
Wadi Midrik
Wadi Beizal
Wadi Sha'it
▼34▼
Silwa Bahari
Nag'el Shibeika
Speos of Horemheb
Kagug
Gebel el Silsileh
160
Faris
Kalabsha
El 'Allani

Gebel Umm Zarabit
709

Wadi Quei
34°E

Bir Quei'

El Hamarawein

▲25▲

1

Gebel Hamrawein
+ 679

Gebel Umm Hammad

El 'Ideid

Bir Nakheil

Bir el 'Anz

38

Al-Quseir

Gebel Umm Balanib
+ 1038

Bir Siyala

El Awetna

Wadi Abu Ziran

R e d

Bir el Muweilih

Bir Kareim

Gebel Hamadat
+ 433

Bir Asal

49

Wadi Kareim

S e a

Wadi Asal

Sharm el Bahari

2

Gebel Umm Khurs
+ 912

Ras Abu 'Aweid

Nasib el Qash
+ 899

Bir Umm Gheig

Al-Bahr al-Ahmar

Gebel Abu Tiyur
1099

Sheikh Malek

Marsa Umm Gheig

Wadi el Arak

Bir Zaidun

+ Gebel el Siba'i
1484

Ras Toronbu

35°15'E

Wadi Zaidun

Marsa Umm Gerifat

24°40'N

Geziret Wadi Gemal

3

Wadi Ma'sar

Wadi el Miyah

Gebel Umm Naqqat
1309 +

Wadi Umm Gheig

Bir Umm Huweitat

Bir el Gindi

Bir Biririq

85

Elphinstone Reef

Marsa Tarafi

4

Wadi Mubarak

Wadi Dubur

Bir el Nuwebi'
787 +

+ Gebel Abu Diab
1160

849
+

Bir Beizah

+ 1096

Marsa 'Alam

Barramiya

Wadi Beizah

75

Gebel 'Igla el Iswid
913 +

Wadi Umm Khariga

42

Marsa 'Alam

Ras Samadai

5

'Urf Umm Rashid
+ 814

Wadi Hafya

Wadi Garf

Bir 'Alam

Marsa Tundaba

Ras Dirra

Bir Dunqash

Samut

Gebel Mudargag
+ 1030

Qalt Umm Kharaba

Hangaliya

Gebel Nugrus
1240 +

Gebel Zabara
+ 1505

Wadi Ghadir

Wadi Muweilha

Migwal el Mafroga

Gebel Hafafit

▼34▼

Wadi Sha'it

Gebel Abu Khruq
955

▼35▼

6

Qalt Umm Sillim

Bir Hileiwat

Gebel Sufra
+ 746

Bir Umm Qubur

Wadi Natash

Bir Abu Had

Wadi Nugrus

Wadi Gemal

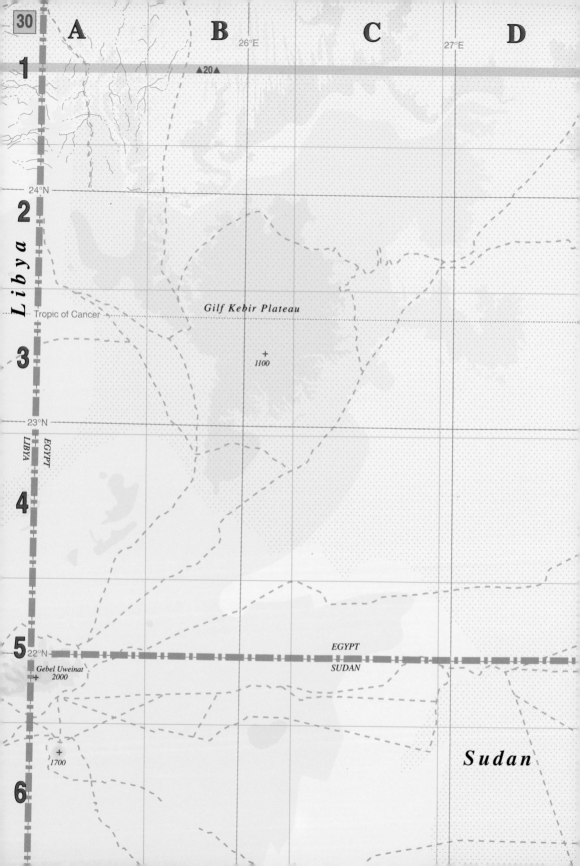

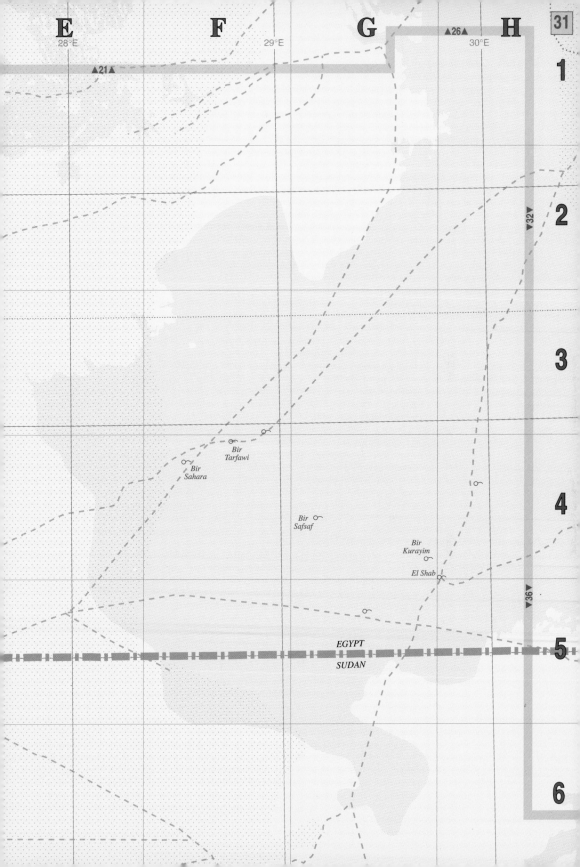

E
28°E

F
29°E

G

H
30°E

▲26▲

▲21▲

1

▼32▼

2

3

Bir
Tarfawi

Bir
Sahara

4

Bir
Safsaf

Bir
Kurayim

El Shab

▼36▼

EGYPT

5

SUDAN

6

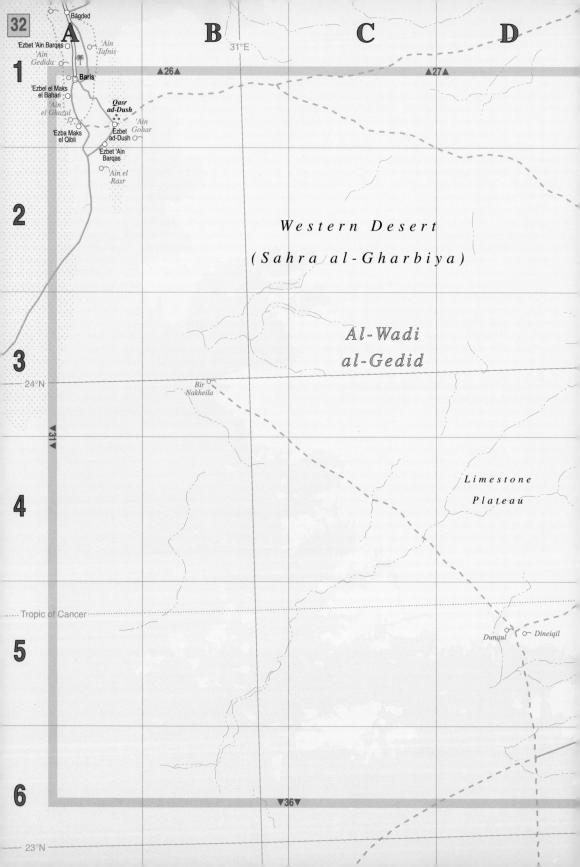

A   B   C   D

Bagded

'Ezbet 'Ain Barqas

'Ain
Gedida

31°E

▲26▲   ▲27▲

1

'Ain
Tafnis

Baris

'Ezbel el Maks
el Bahari

*Qasr
ad-Dush*

'Ain
el Ghazal

Ezbet
ad-Dush

'Ain
Gohar

'Ezba Maks
el Qibli

'Ezbet 'Ain
Barqas

'Ain el
Rasr

2

Western Desert

(Sahra al-Gharbiya)

*Al-Wadi
al-Gedid*

3

24°N

Bir
Nakheila

◄31▼

*Limestone
Plateau*

4

Tropic of Cancer

Dunqul   Dineiqil

5

6

▼36▼

23°N

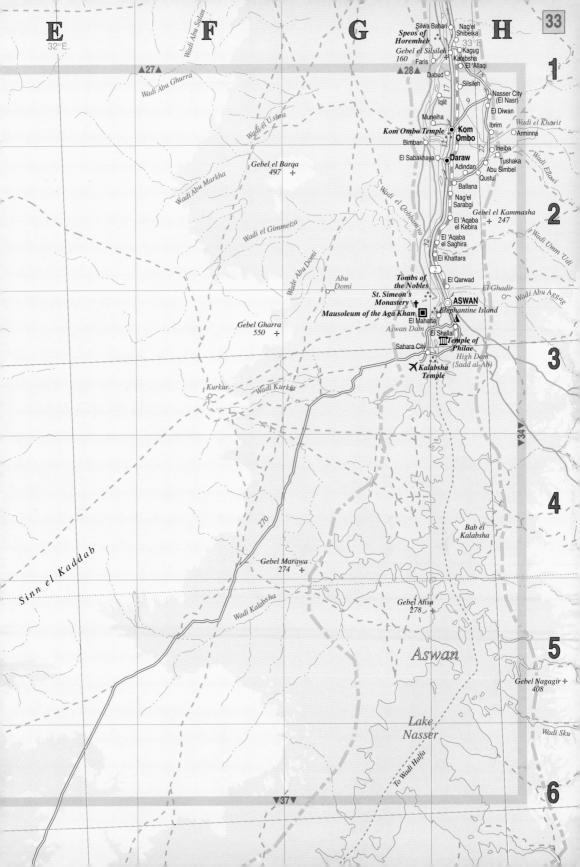

Silwa Bahari Nag'el
Shibeika
Speos of Gebel el Silsileh
Horemheb 160
Faris

Dabud

Silsileh

Iqlit

Muneiha

Kom Ombo Temple ● **Kom**
Ombo

Bimban

El Sabakhaya ● **Daraw**

Adindan

Ballana

Nag'el
Sarabgi

El 'Aqaba
el Kebira

El 'Aqaba
el Saghira

El Khattara

El Qarwad

Tombs of
the Nobles

St. Simeon's
Monastery ✝

Mausoleum of the Aga Khan ▢

El Mahatta

El Shallal

Sahara City

Kalabsha
Temple

Gebel el Barqa
497 +

Gebel Gharra
550 +

Abu
Domi

Kurkur

Wadi Kurkur

270

Sinn el Kaddab

Gebel Marawa
274 +

Wadi Kalabsha

Nag'el

Kagug

Kalabsha

El 'Allaqi

Nasser City
(El Nasr)

El Diwan

Ibrim Arminna

Ineiba

Abu Simbel

Qustul

Gebel el Kammasha
+ 247

El Ghadir

ASWAN

Elephantine Island

Temple of
Philae

High Dam
(Sadd al-Ali)

Wadi el Kharit

Wadi el Allaqi

Tushaka

Wadi Umm 'Udi

Wadi Abu Aggag

Bab el
Kalabsha

Gebel Afisa
278 +

Aswan

Gebel Nagagir +
408

Lake
Nasser

To Wadi Halfa

Wadi Sku

▲27▲ ▲28▲

1

2

3

4

5

6

▼37▼

A   **B**   **C**   **D**

1

2

3

4

5

6

Qalt Umm
Sillim

Bir
Hileiwat

Wadi Sha'it   Gebel Abu Khruq
Gebel Sufra   955
+ 746

Bir Umm Qubur

34°E

Wadi Natash

▲28▲   ▲29▲

Bir
Salama

Bir
Masur

Wadi 'Antar

Wadi el Kharit

Wadi Natash

Bir
Khashal

Wadi Ellawi

Hamret Mukbud
886   +

Bir Ab
Hamam

Wadi Umm 'Udi

Wadi el Lawi

Wadi el Kharit

Wadi Khashab

Bir
Quleib

Rod Kharuf

24° N

Wadi Garara

▼33▼

E a s t e r n   D e s e r t

(S a h r a   a s h - S h a r q i y a)

Wadi el-Quffa

Wadi Raiaiti

Wadi Timsah

Tropic of Cancer

Gebel Na'ag
793   +

Gebel Nagagir
+ 408

Gebel Hadaiyib
716   +

Gebel el Nasiya
994   +

▼38▼

23° N

Wadi Abu Had

E F G H

1

2

3

4

5

6

Bir Abu Had

Wadi Nugrus

Migwal Mukhatatat

35°E

▲29▲

Gebel Musiwirab
+ 1021

Wadi Huluz

Wadi Hamamid

Gebel Abu Hamamid
1745 +

Gebel Hamata
1977 +

Tomb of Sayyid
ash-Shadhili

Gebel Kahfa
1018 +

Bir
Hileiyi

Wadi el Kharit

Gebel Abu Gurdi
1558 +

Gebel Zarqet Na'am
833 +

Wadi el Khiwa

Gebel Umm Bisilla
+ 822

Gebel Dahanib
+ 1268

Al-Bahr
al-Ahmar

Wadi Khuda

Gebel Awamtib
+ 793

Wadi Hodein

Wadi Rahaba

Ras
Honkorab

Wadi Abu Ghusun

Abu Ghusun

Geziret
Siyul

Geziret
Showarit

Gezayir
Mahabis

Wadi Lahemi

44

Old
Forts

Berenice

Kira' el
Hiriwai

Ras
Banas

*Mukawwa
Island*

Foul
Bay

R e d

S e a

Geziret
Mirear

Bir Shalatayn
Bir el Hasa

Marsa
Sha'ab

ADMINISTRATIVE BOUNDARY

44

▼39▼

23°40'N
St John's
Island
Rocky
Island
36°15'E

A   B   C   D

1

23°N   31°E   ▲32▲

W e s t e r n   D e s e r t

(S a h r a   a l - G h a r b i y a)

2

Abu Simbel

Temples of
Abu Simb

*Lake
Nasser*

3

*Al-Wadi
al-Gedid*

Gebel Siri
+ 420

EGYPT

4   23°N   *SUDAN*

Wadi Halfa

5

*Northern
Sudan*

6

Nile River (Bahr el Nil)

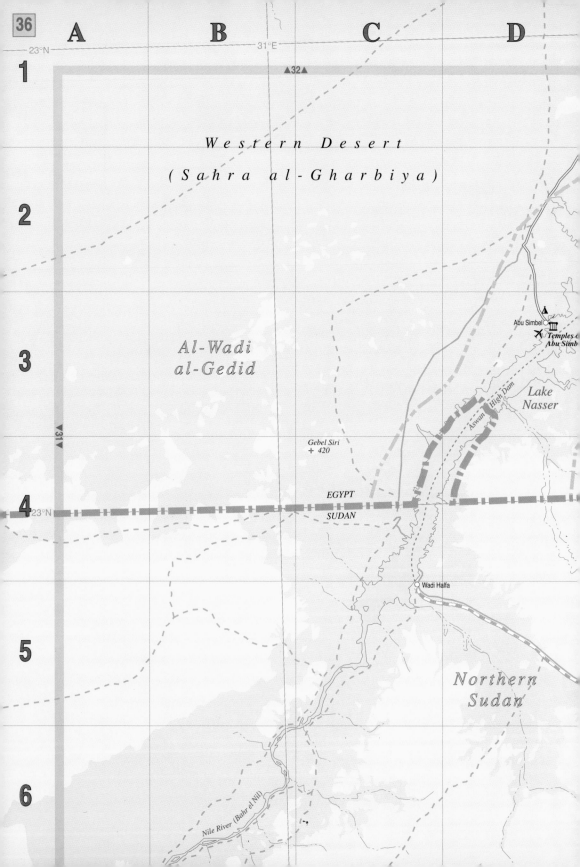

32°E   33°E

1

▲33▲

El Sibu
Temple

Amada
Temple

Lake
Nasser

*Al-Bahr
al-Ahmar*

2

Aswan High Dam · Wadi Halfa

Qasr
Ibrim

Aswan

Wadi Tushka

Wadi el Sibrig

Wadi Hamid

3

Wadi Or

Gebel Nasiya
+ 624

Wadi Kurusku

El 'Aiyinat
595 +

▼38▼

EGYPT

SUDAN

4

S u d a n

N u b i a n   D e s e r t

5

6

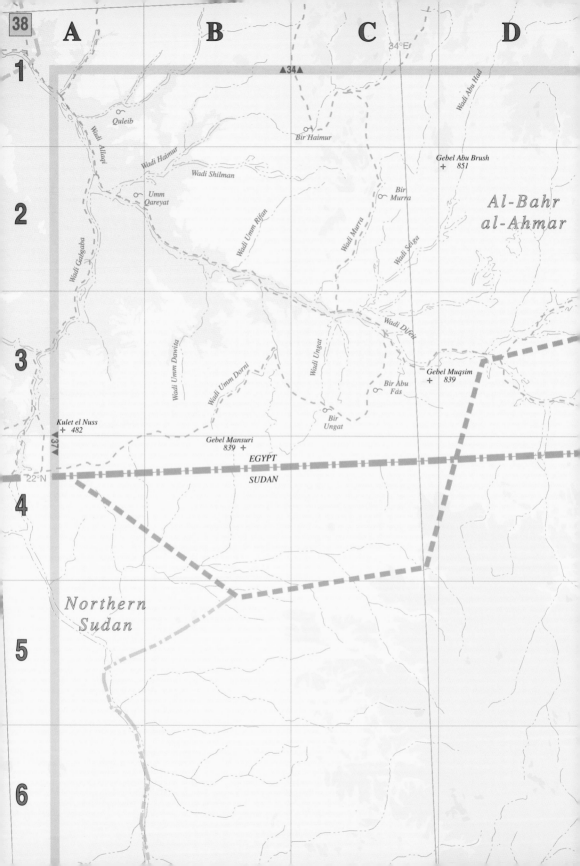

A   B   C   D

1

34°E

▲34▲

Quleib

Bir Haimur

Wadi Allaqi

Wadi Abu Had

Gebel Abu Brush
+ 851

Wadi Haimur

Wadi Shilman

Umm
Qareyat

Bir
Murra

Al-Bahr
al-Ahmar

2

Wadi Gabgaba

Wadi Umm Rifan

Wadi Murra

Wadi Se'iga

Wadi Difeit

3

Wadi Umm Dawita

Wadi Umm Dorni

Wadi Ungat

Bir Abu
Fas

Gebel Muqsim
+ 839

Kulet el Nuss
+ 482

Bir
Ungat

Gebel Mansuri
839 +

EGYPT

SUDAN

22°N

4

Northern
Sudan

5

6

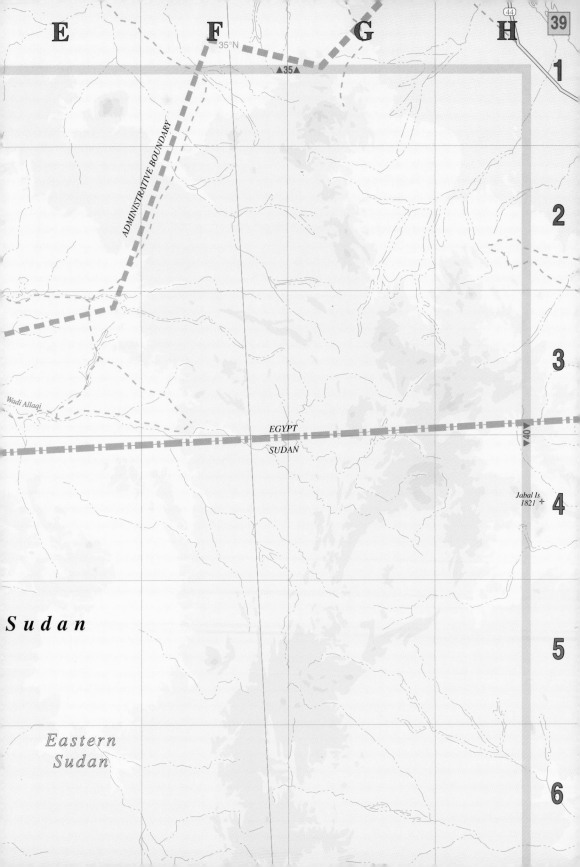

35°N

▲35▲

ADMINISTRATIVE BOUNDARY

Wadi Allaqi

EGYPT

SUDAN

▲40▼
▲

Jabal Is
1821 +

S u d a n

*Eastern
Sudan*

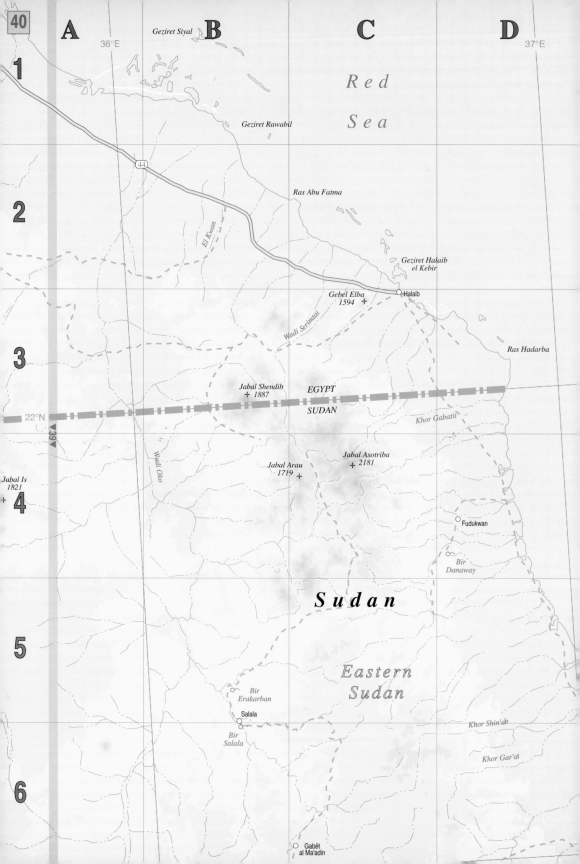

A B C D

36°E

37°E

1

Geziret Siyal

R e d

S e a

Geziret Rawabil

44

Ras Abu Fatma

2

El Kwan

*Geziret Halaib
el Kebir*

Gebel Elba
1594 ✛

○ Halaib

Wadi Serimtai

Ras Hadarba

3

Jabal Shendib
✛ *1887*

EGYPT

SUDAN

Khor Gabatit

22°N

▼39▼

Wadi Oko

Jabal Arau
1719 ✛

Jabal Asotriba
✛ *2181*

Jabal Is
1821
✛

4

○ *Fudukwan*

○○ *Bir*
Danaway

S u d a n

5

Eastern

Sudan

○ *Bir*
Erakarban

○ *Salala*
○○

Khor Shin'ab

Bir
Salala

Khor Gar'at

6

○ *Gabêt*
al Ma'adin

TONY WHEELER

LEANNE LOGAN

LEANNE LOGAN

LEANNE LOGAN

Top: Towering minarets of Islamic Cairo
Middle: Feluccas near Aswan
Bottom: The sublime artwork inside the Tomb of Nefertari, Valley of the Queens, near Luxor

Getting Around Egypt

Bus

Various bus companies operate in Egypt and, combined, they provide cheap and very reliable transport to virtually every nook and cranny of the country. Tickets are usually bought at ticket booths, or on the bus itself. Depending on the route, seats can be booked in advance, which is a wise idea on the more popular runs, eg Cairo to Alexandria or Suez to Sharm el-Sheikh. There are no student discounts.

Buses come in two types – deluxe services of the Superjet variety, and the ordinary old local heaps.

Deluxe buses tend to offer non-stop (or few stops) service between many main cities and towns. The more comfortable of these buses boast loud videos (bring ear plugs if you're not into Egyptian soap operas), air conditioning (which tends to get very cold on overnight trips), and a toilet. On some runs there's even an (expensive) on-board snack service. Despite displaying 'no smoking' signs, these buses are usually chock-full of cigarette smoke.

Local buses service both short and long distances, and are usually dusty, uncomfortable and very crowded.

LEANNE LOGAN
Traditionally clad Bedouin woman at a street market in Al-Arish, Sinai

Buses are generally safe to travel in, although journeying at night can be dangerous as accidents are not uncommon. Breakdowns are also par for the course.

Train

Egypt's railway network runs almost the length of the country and, for those prepared to travel in 3rd class, it's the cheapest way to get around. For travellers whose visit is limited to a trip up and down the Nile Valley and who can afford a 2nd-class ticket, it is also one of the most comfortable, if not the fastest, means of travel. Punctuality, however, is not guaranteed.

At the top of the range are the luxurious and relatively expensive sleeper trains, known as Wagon-Lits, which boast double compartments and meals on-board. Next up are the air-conditioned 1st & 2nd-class trains, which make limited stops and have comfortable cushioned seats. These are followed by the slower non-air-con 2nd-class trains and, at the bottom of the barrel, 3rd-class wagons. The latter tend to be crammed full of people and belongings, all precariously piled onto hard wooden benches. Vendors constantly ply the aisles selling food and drinks and, although progress can be slow on these trains, you should eventually get to your destination – *insha-allah*.

Fares are very reasonable, even ultra cheap compared with train travel in Western countries. Also, the big advantage of trains over buses is that there is a student discount (of up to 50%), providing you have an International Student Identification Card (ISIC). Seats in 1st and 2nd-class air-con trains can be reserved in advance, and on some routes (Cairo to Luxor in particular) this is a must.

Road

Roads in Egypt are not the exclusive reserve of motor vehicles. Dodging camels, donkey carts, children and chickens is all part and parcel of driving in Egypt and, for the inexperienced, it can be quite a hairraising ordeal. Driving at night is not recommended.

On the whole, the road network is good and most major roads are sealed. Traffic is not too heavy, apart from in the major cities where it can appear to be chaotic. Petrol is a mere E£1 a litre.

Rentacar companies have offices in Cairo, Alexandria and the major tourist destinations. You'll need your International Driving Permit and you should be over 25 years of age to rent a vehicle.

Service taxis, either in the form of a seven-seater Peugeot 504 or a minibus (often referred to as a microbus), weave their way all around the country (though they're less common in the Sinai). They leave when full and are generally faster than either buses or trains, but a little more expensive. Hiring one of these for yourself is much dearer still, as it then becomes known as a 'Special'.

Bicycle

Considering the heat, sand and crowds, biking is only an option for short trips, eg for getting around Luxor, Aswan and the oases. Bikes are available for hire in some hotels or bike shops for around E£5 a day.

Camel

Gliding over sand dunes or through desert wadis on camelback is one of the most intimate ways of getting to know what many would call the 'real Egypt'. Camel treks can be limited to a or e-hour jaunt around the Pyramids of Giza, or extended to a week-long safari in the Western Desert or the Sinai. Count on paying about E£50 a day for your ship of the desert and a guide.

Hantours & Caretas

Horse or donkey-drawn carriages, known as hantours and caretas respectively, are available for sightseeing purposes in some towns. In a few places, they're also still used as public transport. Hantours are mainly found in cities, while caretas tend to be used only in Marsa Matruh and Siwa.

Boat

Flotels and feluccas are the two main modes of transport on the Nile, Egypt's only river.

Flotels, or floating hotels, are four or five-star luxury cruisers which cater mainly to package holiday-makers on voyages between Cairo and Aswan. They're designed for those who want to let Egypt and her crowds sedately pass by.

Feluccas are the ancient sailboats of the Nile and, without doubt, they are one of the country's unique attractions. A sunset sail is a must for any visitor to Cairo, Luxor or, ideally, Aswan. Those with a few days and nights up their sleeve will find nothing more relaxing than a voyage from Aswan to Edfu on one of these graceful little boats.

There is a ferry from Hurghada to Sharm el-Sheikh every second day, but the crossing can be pretty rough.

GEERT COLE

Mosque at Marsa Matruh on the Mediterranean coast

Comment Circuler en Égypte

Bus

L'Égypte compte plusieurs compagnies sérieuses de transport en bus qui permettent de se rendre à peu de frais dans les coins les plus reculés du pays. En général, les billets se vendent soit au guichet soit directement dans le bus. Sur certains trajets, il est possible de réserver sa place, ce qui est fortement conseillé sur les lignes les plus fréquentées, notamment entre Le Caire et Alexandrie ou Suez et Charm el-Cheikh. Aucune réduction n'est accordée aux étudiants.

Il existe deux types de bus : les services de luxe modernes et les bons vieux tacots locaux. Le plus souvent, les premiers assurent des liaisons directes (ou avec peu d'arrêts) entre les grandes villes. Les plus confortables sont dotés de TV bruyantes sur lesquelles vous pouvez suivre des mélos égyptiens en vidéo (prévoyez des boules Quiès si vous n'êtes pas un amateur). Ils sont également équipés de systèmes de climatisation (il peut d'ailleurs faire assez froid sur les trajets de nuit) et de toilettes. Certains proposent même un service de vente ambulante (à prix élevé). Même s'il est indiqué qu'il est interdit de fumer, il règne généralement une atmosphère enfumée. Si les services de bus locaux assurent aussi bien les liaisons longue distance que les trajets courts, ils offrent souvent un confort rudimentaire (sièges peu rembourrés) et sont aussi poussiéreux que bondés.

En règle générale, les voyages en bus sont plutôt sûrs ; les trajets de nuit sont néanmoins parfois ponctués d'accidents, sans oublier les pannes relativement fréquentes.

Train

Le réseau ferroviaire égyptien couvre pratiquement l'ensemble du pays et, pour ceux qui sont prêts à voyager en 3e classe, le train reste le moyen de transport le moins onéreux. Pour les visiteurs dont le séjour se limite à la descente ou la remontée de la vallée du Nil et qui ont les moyens de s'offrir un billet de 2e classe, c'est également le moyen le plus confortable, même si ce n'est pas le plus rapide, de se déplacer. La ponctualité n'est toutefois pas garantie.

Dans la gamme supérieure, les couchettes, ou wagon-lits, se targuent d'offrir à leurs passagers un compartiment double ainsi qu'un service de restauration à bord. Ensuite viennent les trains de 1re et 2e classes climatisés, qui s'arrêtent peu et sont pourvus de confortables sièges matelassés. Les trains de 2e classe non climatisés sont un peu plus lents. Au bas de l'échelle, les voitures de 3e classe sont souvent bondées. Les passagers s'entassent avec leurs effets personnels sur d'inconfortables bancs en bois tandis que les vendeurs ambulants tentent de se frayer un chemin dans les allées. Malgré la lenteur de ces trains, vous êtes quasiment assuré – *inch' Allah* ! – d'arriver à destination.

BETHUNE CARMICHAEL

BETHUNE CARMICHAEL

Left: Mosque of Sultan Mu'ayyad Sheikh, Cairo
Right: Sugar cane farming in Sohag, the Nile Valley

Les billets sont bon marché, même donnés par rapport aux tarifs pratiqués dans les pays occidentaux. Le train présente en outre l'énorme avantage pour les étudiants de bénéficier d'une réduction (jusqu'à 50%), à condition qu'ils soient en possession de la carte étudiante internationale. Il est possible de réserver sa place sur les trains de 1re et 2e classes climatisés ; sur certaines lignes (Le Caire-Louxor, en particulier), c'est d'ailleurs hautement recommandé.

Route

En Égypte, la route n'est pas le domaine réservé des véhicules motorisés. Les chameaux côtoient les poules et les charrettes tirées par des ânes. Les conducteurs qui n'ont pas l'habitude de ce genre de situation trouveront sans doute l'expérience un peu pénible. En tous cas, il est déconseillé de rouler la nuit. Dans l'ensemble, le réseau routier est en bon état et la plupart des routes principales sont bitumées. La circulation n'est pas trop dense, en dehors des grandes villes où il semble régner un véritable chaos. Le litre d'essence ne coûte guère plus d'une livre égyptienne. Les agences de location de voitures sont représentées au Caire, à Alexandrie ainsi que dans toutes les villes touristiques. Pour louer un véhicule, il faut avoir plus de 25 ans et présenter un permis de conduire international. Les taxis, qu'il s'agisse de 504 Peugeot à sept places ou de minibus (souvent appelés microbus), sillonnent tout le pays (néanmoins ils sont moins courants dans le Sinaï). Ils ne partent qu'une fois pleins et vont généralement plus vite que les bus ou le train, mais ils coûtent un peu plus cher. La location d'un taxi privé vous reviendra encore plus cher car il s'agit dans ce cas d'un "spécial".

GLENN BEANLAND

Queen Hatshepsut's Temple in Luxor

Bicyclette

Compte tenu de la chaleur, du sable et de la circulation, mieux vaut réserver ce moyen de transport aux trajets courts, notamment pour la visite des environs de Louxor, d'Assouan ou des oasis. Les vélos se louent dans certains hôtels ainsi que dans les magasins de cycles à 50 livres égyptiennes par jour.

Chameau

Traverser les dunes ou les wadis du désert à dos de chameau est sans doute le moyen le plus adapté de découvrir ce que d'aucuns appellent "l'Égypte authentique". Vous pouvez opter pour la formule d'une heure de promenade autour des pyramides de Gizeh ou entreprendre une véritable expédition d'une semaine dans le désert de Libye ou dans le Sinaï. Comptez environ 50 livres égyptiennes par jour pour votre vaisseau du désert et son guide.

Hantour et careta

Dans certaines villes, il est possible de découvrir les curiosités touristiques à bord d'attelages tirés par des chevaux ou des ânes, que l'on appelle respectivement hantours et caretas.

Les premiers sont plutôt l'apanage des villes tandis que les seconds semblent n'exister qu'à Marsa Matrouh et Siouah.

Bateau

Les flotels et les felouques sont les deux principaux moyens de transport pour circuler sur le Nil, l'unique fleuve d'Égypte.

Les flotels, ou hôtels flottants, sont des bateaux de luxe de quatre à cinq étoiles qui prennent essentiellement en charge les groupes de vacanciers en voyage organisé du Caire à Assouan. Ils sont conçus pour ceux qui préfèrent observer le pays et la foule de ses habitants à distance.

Les felouques, traditionnelles embarcations à voile sont sans aucun doute l'une des principales curiosités du pays. Tout visiteur se rendant au Caire, à Louxor ou mieux à Assouan se doit d'assister au coucher du soleil sur l'un de ces gracieux voiliers. Pour se détendre, ceux qui disposent de peu de temps ne trouveront pas mieux que de voguer ainsi d'Assouan à Edfou. Un bac permet de traverser de Hourghada à Charm el-Cheikh tous les deux jours, mais la traversée est parfois très mauvaise.

Reisen in Ägypten

Bus

Verschiedene Busunternehmen sind in Ägypten tätig. In Kombination sorgen sie für billigen und sehr zuverlässigen Transport in praktisch jeden Winkel des Landes. Tickets kann man in der Regel an Fahrkartenständen oder im Bus selbst kaufen. Abhängig von der Route kann man Plätze im voraus buchen, was auf den beliebteren Strecken empfehlenswert ist, z.B. von Kairo nach Alexandria oder von Suez nach Sharm as-Shaykh. Studentenermäßigungen gibt es nicht.

Man findet zwei Bustypen: Luxuslinien in der Art des Superjets und die einfachen alten Karren der Gegend.

Luxusbusse fahren zwischen vielen wichtigen Städten und Orten non-stop (oder mit wenigen Stationen). Die komfortableren dieser Busse sind mit lauten Videos (Ohrenstöpsel sind ratsam, wenn man nicht auf Ägyptische Seifenopern steht), Klimaanlage (die bei Übernachtfahrten sehr kalt werden kann) und einer Toilette ausgestattet. Auf einigen Strecken ist sogar ein (teurer) Snackservice an Bord. Trotz der Rauchverbot-Schilder sind diese Busse üblicherweise voller Zigarettenqualm.

Die lokalen Busdienste decken sowohl kurze als auch lange Strecken ab. Sie sind jedoch meist einfach ausgestattet (schlecht gepolsterte Sitze), staubig und sehr voll.

Busse sind im Allgemeinen eine sichere Reiseart. Fahrten bei Nacht können jedoch gefährlich sein, da Unfälle nicht unüblich sind. Auch Pannen sind an der Tagesordnung.

Zug

Ägyptens Bahnnetz deckt fast die gesamte Länge des Landes ab. Wenn man bereit ist, dritte Klasse zu reisen, ist es die billigste Art, herumzukommen. Für Reisende, deren Besuch auf eine Rundfahrt durch das Niltal beschränkt ist und die sich eine Fahrkarte 2. Klaße leisten können, ist dies eine der bequemsten, wahrscheinlich sogar die schnellste Art zu reisen. Pünktlichkeit ist aber dennoch nicht garantiert.

An der Spitze stehen die luxuriösen und relativ teuren Schlafwagen, bekannt als Wagon-Lits, welche Zweierabteile und Mahlzeiten an Bord führen. Danach kommen die 1. und 2. Klasse-Züge, die mit Klimaanlage ausgestattet sind, nur selten halten und bequem gepolsterte Sitze haben. Dann folgen die langsameren 2. Klasse-Züge ohne Klimaanlage. Und am unteren Ende die 3. Klasse Waggons. Letztere sind häufig vollgestopft mit Menschen und Gepäck, abenteuerlich auf die harten Holzbänke gestapelt. Händler, die Essen und Trinken verkaufen, pendeln ständig die Gänge auf und ab. Auch wenn die Fahrt mit diesen Zügen sehr langsam sein kann, gelangt man schließlich an sein Ziel – *inshallah*.

Die Fahrpreise sind sehr günstig, ja sogar superbillig im Vergleich zu Bahnreisen in westlichen Ländern. Und außerdem haben die Züge gegenüber den Bussen den großen Vorteil, daß eine Studentenermäßigung (bis zu 50%) gewährt wird. Vorausgesetzt, man besitzt einen internationalen Studentenausweis (ISIC). Platzreservierungen

Temple of Hathor, Abu Simbel

GLENN BEANLAND

in den klimatisierten 1. und 2. Klasse-Zügen sind möglich und auf manchen Strecken (insbesondere von Kairo nach Luxor) unerläßlich.

Straße

Die Straßen in Ägypten gehören nicht nur den Kraftfahrzeugen. Das Ausweichen vor Kamelen, Eselkarren, Kindern und Hühnern ist wesentlicher Bestandteil des Fahrens in Ägypten, so daß es besonders für Unerfahrene zur haarsträubenden Tortur werden kann. Nachtfahrten sind nicht zu empfehlen.

Im Großen und Ganzen ist das Straßennetz gut und die meisten Hauptstraßen sind asphaltiert. Der Verkehr ist nicht zu stark, abgesehen von den größeren Städten, wo es chaotisch zugehen kann. Benzin kostet nur 1 E£ pro Liter.

Autovermietungen haben Büros in Kairo, Alexandria und den wichtigsten Reisezielen. Sie benötigen einen internationalen Führerschein und sollten über 25 Jahre alt sein, um ein Auto zu mieten.

Miettaxen, als Sieben-Sitzer Peugeot 504 oder als Minibus (häufig als Microbus bezeichnet) winden sich durch das ganze Land (obgleich seltener im Sinai). Sobald sie voll sind fahren sie los und sind im Allgemeinen schneller als Busse oder Züge, allerdings ein bischen teurer. Wenn man sich eines dieser Taxis exklusiv mietet, wird es nochmal um einiges teurer, da es dann zur "Sonderfahrt" wird.

Fahrrad

In Anbetracht der Hitze, des Sandes und der Menschenmengen, stellt Fahrrad fahren nur für kürzere Strecken eine Alternative dar. Um z.B. in Luxor, Assuan und in den Oasen herumzukommen. Fahrräder kann man in manchen Hotels oder in Fahrradgeschäften für etwa 5 E£ am Tag ausleihen.

Kamel

Auf dem Rücken eines Kamels über Sanddünen oder durch Wüsten Wadis zu gleiten ist eine der intimsten Arten, das, was viele das 'wahre Ägypten' nennen, kennenzulernen. Kamel-Trecks können auf einen einstündigen Ausflug um die Pyramiden von Gizeh begrenzt sein. Oder auf eine einwöchige Safari in die westliche Wüste oder ins Sinai ausgedehnt werden. Rechnen Sie mit etwa 50 E£ am Tag für das Wüstenschiff inklusive Führer.

Hantours & Caretas

Pferde oder Eselkutschen, beziehungsweise die sogenannten Hantours und Caretas, stehen in manchen Städten für Sightseeing-Zwecke zur Verfügung. An wenigen Orten werden sie auch immer noch als öffentliche Verkehrsmittel genutzt. Hantours findet man hauptsächlich in den Städten, während Caretas vorwiegend in Marsa Matru und Siwa benutzt werden.

Boot

Flotels und Feluccas sind die zwei Haupttransportmittel auf dem Nil, Ägyptens einzigem Fluß.

Flotels, oder schwimmende Hotels, sind vier bis fünf-Sterne Luxuskreuzer, die vor allem Pauschalurlauber auf der Reise zwischen Kairo und Aßuan beherbergen. Sie sind für diejenigen bestimmt, die Ägypten und seine Menschen ruhig an sich vorbeiziehen lassen wollen.

Feluccas sind die altertümlichen Segelboote auf dem Nil. Zweifelsohne gehören sie zu den einzigartigen Attraktionen des Landes. Ein Segeltrip bei Sonnenuntergang ist ein Muß für jeden Besucher in Kairo, Luxor, oder, idealerweise, in Assuan. Für diejenigen, die einige Tage und Nächte in petto haben, gibt es nichts entspannenderes als eine Reise von Assuan nach Idfu auf einem dieser stolzen kleinen Boote.

Zwischen Hurghada und Sharm ash-Shaykh verkehrt alle zwei Tage eine Fähre, aber die Überfahrt kann rauh sein.

GREG ELMS

In the market for a camel?

Cómo Movilizarse dentro de Egipto

En Autobús

En Egipto operan varias compañías de autobuses y, combinadas, ofrecen transporte barato y efectivo a todos los rincones y escondrijos del país. Por lo general, los pasajes se compran en taquillas especiales o en el mismo autobús. Según la ruta, los asientos pueden reservarse con anticipación, lo que es una buena idea en las rutas más populares, por ejemplo del Cairo a Alejandría o de Suez a Sharm el-Sheikh. No se ofrecen descuentos a los estudiantes.

Los autobuses son de dos tipos – Los de lujo, de la variedad Superjet, y los viejos y anticuados locales.

Los autobuses de lujo ofrecen servicios sin paradas

LEANNE LOGAN

Horus – a detail of the Temple of Philae, Aswan

(o con pocas paradas) entre muchas ciudades y poblaciones importantes. Los de más confort tienen videos a todo volumen (si a usted no le encantan las películas egipcias le aconsejamos que se traiga tapones para las orejas), aire acondicionado (que tiende a enfriar mucho el ambiente durante los viajes nocturnos), y sanitario. En algunas rutas incluso tienen un servicio (caro) de comidas ligeras. A pesar de los anuncios "prohibido fumar", por lo general, estos autobuses están llenos de humo de cigarrillo.

Los autobuses locales sirven las distancias cortas y las largas, pero, por lo general, son de comodidad básica (asientos con poco acojina-miento), polvorientos y muy apiñados.

Por lo general, en los autobuses se viaja sin peligro personal, pero los viajes nocturnos pueden ser peligrosos ya que los accidentes son frecuentes. Las averías son también parte de la aventura.

En Tren

El ferrocarril de Egipto prácticamente recorre casi todo el largo del país y, para los que estén dispuestos a viajar en 3ª clase, es el medio de transporte más barato. Además, para los viajeros que tienen que limitarse a un viaje de ida y vuelta a lo largo del Valle del Nilo y pueden pagar un pasaje de 2ª clase, es uno de los medios de transporte más cómodos, aunque no el más rápido. No se garantiza la puntualidad.

En el grado más alto están los lujosos y relativamente caros trenes con literas conocidos como Wagon-Lits, que se jactan de tener compartimientos dobles y comidas a bordo. Luego están los trenes climatizados con vagones de 1ª

y 2ª clase que hacen pocas paradas y tienen asientos acojinados. Siguen los trenes más lentos y sin aire acondicionado con vagones de 2ª clase y, en el grado más bajo de la escala, los vagones de 3ª clase. Estos últimos tienden a estar apiñados de gente y sus pertenencias, todo amontonado en forma precaria encima de banquillos de madera. Por los pasillos pasan constante-mente vendedores de comidas y bebidas y, aunque en estos trenes el avance es lento, eventualmente llegará a su destino —Insha-Alá.

Los pasajes son a precio razonable, incluso baratísimos si se comparan con los precios del mundo occidental. Además, la gran ventaja que tienen los trenes comparándolos con los autobuses es el descuento que ofrecen a los estudiantes (hasta de un 50%), siempre y cuando usted tenga un Carnet Internacional de Identidad Estudiantil (ISIC). Los asientos de 1ª y 2ª de los trenes climatizados pueden reservarse por adelantado y en algunas rutas (del Cairo a Luxor en particular) esto es indispensable.

Por Carretera

En Egipto, las carreteras no son de uso exclusivo de los automotores. Para manejar en Egipto hay que dominar el arte de saber esquivar los camellos, las carretas tiradas por asnos, los niños y las gallinas, lo que a los que no tienen experiencia puede que les haga poner los pelos de punta. No se recomienda manejar por la noche.

En general, las carreteras son buenas y la mayoría de las principales están asfaltadas. El tráfico no es muy pesado, aparte de las ciudades más grandes donde da la impresión de ser caótico. La gasolina cuesta solamente £E 1 por litro.

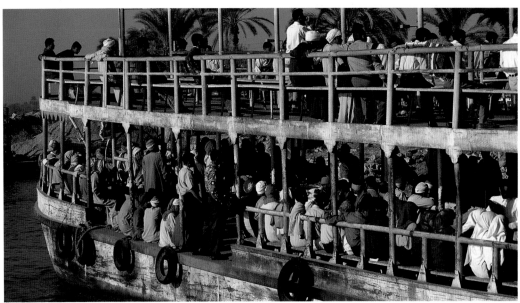

LEANNE LOGAN

A crowded public ferry plies the Nile at Luxor

Las compañías de coches de alquiler tienen oficinas en El Cairo, Alejandría y los centros de destinación turística más importantes. Usted necesitará su Licencia Internacional de Conducir y para alquilar un vehículo tiene que haber cumplido los 25 años de edad.

Los servicios de taxis, bien con automóviles Peugeot 504 de siete plazas o con minibuses (conocidos también por microbuses), serpentean por todo el país (aunque menos en la zona del Sinaí). Parten cuando se llenan y por lo general son más rápidos que los autobuses y los trenes, pero son un poco más caros. Si se alquila para uno solo aún sale más caro, y entonces se le llama 'Especial'.

En Bicicleta

Teniendo en cuenta el calor, la arena y las muchedumbres, la bicicleta es sólo una opción para viajes cortos, por ejemplo para desplazarse por Luxor, Aswan y los oasis. Pueden alquilarse bicicletas en algunos hoteles y en las tiendas de bicicletas por unas £E 5, por día.

En Camello

Deslizarse sobre las dunas o por los uadis del desierto a espaldas de un camello es una de las maneras más íntimas de conocer lo que muchos llamarían "el Egipto real". Los recorridos en camello pueden limitarse a una hora por los alrededores de las pirámides de Giza, o extenderse a un safari de una semana de duración en el Desierto del Oeste o en el del Sinaí. Calcule que le costará unas £E 50 por día por la nave del desierto y el guía.

Hantours y Caretas

A los carruajes tirados por caballos y burros se les conoce por hantours y caretas respectivamente y en algunas poblaciones se pueden obtener para dar un paseo. En algunos pocos lugares todavía se usan como medio de transporte público. Los hantours se encuentran principalmente en las ciudades, mientras que las caretas se usan casi solamente en Marsa Matruh Siwa.

En Bote

Los floteles y las felúas son las dos formas principales de transporte en el Nilo, el único río de Egipto.

Los floteles, u hoteles flotantes, son cruceros de lujo de cinco y seis estrellas que por lo general atienden a los turistas con viajes organizados entre las ciudades de Cairo y Aswan. Están diseñados para los que quieran pasar de lado, de manera sedada, Egipto y sus aglomeraciones de gente.

Las felúas son las antiguas embarcaciones a vela del Nilo y, sin duda, son una de las atracciones más interesantes del país. Los visitantes del Cairo, Luxor y, preferiblemente, Aswan no deben perderse un viaje en felúa a la puesta del sol. Los que puedan disponer de algunos días y noches encontrarán muy placentero un viaje desde Aswan a Edfu en una de esas lindas embarcaciones.

Cada dos días hay un transbordador de Hurghada a Sharm el-Skeikh pero el cruce puede ser bastante turbulento.

エジプトの旅

バス

エジプトにはバス会社がいろいろあって国内を隅々まで結び、安くて信頼のおける交通手段を提供している。乗車券は通常、切符売り場かバスの車内で買う。路線によっては座席を予約することができる。カイロ（Cairo）、アレキサンドリア（Alexandria）間や、スエズ（Suez）、シャームエルシェイク（Sharm el-Sheikh）間などの混雑しやすい路線を使う時は、あらかじめ座席を予約しておいたほうがいい。学生割引はない。

バスには2つのタイプがある。ひとつは高速（スーパージェットSuperjet）のデラックスタイプ、もうひとつは古いぽんこつのローカルタイプ。

デラックスバスは主要都市をノンストップ（またはほとんど停車しない）で走っていることが多い。その中でも特に乗り心地のいいとされるバスの車内には、ビデオ（たいへんうるさいので、エジプトの恋愛ドラマに興味がない人は耳栓を持っていくといい）、冷房（夜行だととても寒くなることがある）、トイレが設置されている。いくつかの路線には、スナック類の車内販売（高い）もある。「禁煙」のサインが表示してあるにもかかわらず、ほとんどの場合、車内はたばこの煙でいっぱいだ。

ローカルバスには短距離、長距離両方あるが、設備は最小限（パッドが薄い座席）で、埃っぽく、たいへん込んでいる。

一般的にバスの旅行は安全だが、夜行だと事故が多い。故障は日常茶飯事だ。

電車

エジプトの鉄道網は国を南北に通っている。3等列車で旅行する覚悟のある人にとっては、最も安い手段だ。ナイル渓谷を南北に旅行するだけを目的とし、2等席を買う余裕のある人にとっては、もっとも楽な移動方法のひとつである。しかし、遅くて時間には正確ではない。

最高級の電車は、ワゴン・リット（Wagon-Lit）の名で知られている、豪華で料金が割高の寝台列車だ。これはダブルサイズの仕切り客室で食事付き。その次のクラスは冷房付きの1等、2等列車で、停車駅が少なく座席も座り心地がいい。その下クラスは遅くて冷房なしの2等列車、そして最も低い3等ワゴン列車。これらは木製の硬いベンチに不安定に積み上げられた荷物と乗客とでごった返していることが多い。つねに売人が食べ物や飲み物を売りに通路を往復する。このような電車での旅行は遅いけれども目的地には必ず到着できる（アラーのおぼしめししならば）。

エジプトのどのクラスの電車料金も西洋諸国と比べるととても安い。電車旅行の利点は、国際学生証（ISIC）があれば、学生割引（最高50%まで）がきくことだ。バスにはこの制度はない。1等、2等列車は予約可能。いくつかのルート、特にカイロ、ルクソル（Luxor）間は予約が必要だ。

道路

エジプトの道路は自動車以外にもさまざまなものが往

LEANNE LOGAN

Sinai road scene

LEANNE LOGAN

Khan al-Khalili Bazaar, Cairo

来している。道を横切るラクダ、ロバが引く荷車、子供、ニワトリなど、すべてがエジプトの自動車旅行に伴う。運転経験の浅い人には身の毛が弥立つ試練となる。夜間の運転は避けたほうがいい。

道路交通網は全体的によく発達していて幹線道路はほとんど舗装されている。主要都市内の大混乱を除けば道路はあまり込んでいない。ガソリンは1リットルたったのE£1だ。

レンタカー会社はカイロ、アレキサンドリア、その他の観光都市で事務所を開いている。25才以上で、国際免許がないとレンタカーを借りることはできない。

タクシーとして、7座席のプジョー 504、またはミニバス（マイクロバスとも呼ばれる）が、国中を走っている（シナイ半島では比較的少ない）。満席になると出発するが、一般的にバスや電車より速く、料金が少し高い。これらは借り切ることができるが「スペシャル」と呼ばれ、その名の通り料金が高い。

自転車

熱気、砂、人ごみなどを考慮に入れると、自転車は、ルクソル、アスワン（Aswan）、オアシスなど、短距離の旅行方法のひとつとして考えたほうがいい。自転車はいくつかのホテルや自転車屋で1日E£5程度で借りられる。

ラクダ

多くの人々が語る「本当のエジプト」を深く知るもっともいい旅行の方法は、ラクダの背に乗って砂丘を越え、砂漠のワジを渡ることだ。ラクダでのトレッキングは、ギザのピラミッド（Pyramids of Giza）周辺を1時間ほど遠足するものから、ウェスタン砂漠（Western Desert）、またはシナイ半島を1週間サファリするものまである。砂漠での乗り賃とガイド料を含めて1日E£50程度を考えておくこと。

馬車とロバ車

馬、またはロバに引かせる客車はそれぞれハントゥア（hantours）、カリタ（caretas）と呼ばれ、いくつかの街で観光に用いることができる。2、3の街では、今でも公共交通手段として使用されている。ハントゥアはおもに都市で使われているが、カリタはマルサマトルー（Marsa Matruh）とシーワ（Siwa）にしかない。

ボート

エジプト唯一の川、ナイル川のおもな交通機関は、フローテル（flotels）とフェルッカ（feluccas）だ。

フローテル、もしくは水上ホテルは4つ星または5つ星の豪華客船で、パック旅行客を中心にカイロからアスワンまでの船旅を提供している。これはエジプトとエジプト人の群集を素通りしたい旅行者のためにデザインされている。

フェルッカはナイル川古来の帆船で、文句なしにこの国のユニークなアトラクションのひとつだ。カイロ、ルクソル、特にアスワンの日没時の船旅は特におすすめ。数日間、旅行する余裕のある人にとって、この小さく美しい船に乗ってアスワンからイドフ（Edfu）まで行く旅ほどリラックスできるものはない。

フルガダ（Hurghada）からシャームエルシェイクまではフェリーが2日毎に運航しているが、渡航は荒れる。

GEERT COLE

Bedouin men on Dahab beach

Index

NATIONAL PARKS

OASES

RAILWAY STATIONS

RUINS & PYRAMIDS

Khalig el Tina 13 H2
Khor Gabatit (S) 40 C3
Khor Gar'at (S) 40 D6
Khor Shin'ab (S) 40 D6
Kira'el Hiriwai 35 G2
Lake Nasser 33 G6, 36 D3
Little Bitter Lake (Buheirat Murrat el
   Sughra) 13 H5
Magal el Dob 24 D5
Marsa 'Alam 29 H5
Marsa Abu Makhadiq 25 E4
Marsa Bareika 25 F2
Marsa el Hamra 11 G2
Marsa Tarafi 29 G4
Marsa Tundaba 29 H5
Marsa Umm Gerifat 29 G3
Marsa Umm Gheig 29 G3
Masabb Dumyat 13 F1
Masabb Rashid 12 B1
Masraf el Gharbiya el Raisi 12 D1
Mersa Thilmet 18 A3
Mukawwa Island 35 H3
Nahal el Ha' Arava (J) 15 H3
Nahal Be'er Sheva' (I) 15 G1
Nahal Lavan (I) 15 F2
Nahal Nizana (I) 15 F3
Nahal Paran (I) 15 G4
Nahal Zenifim (I) 15 G5
Nasib Sa'd 11 G2
Nile River (Bahr el Nil) (S) 36 B6
Nile River (Bahr el Nil) 17 E3, 23 E5,
   27 G1, 28 A5
Qad Ibn Haddan 25 E2
Qana el Manzala 13 F1
Qar'a el Ibrahimfya 22 D3
Qar'a el Nubariya 12 B3
Quleib 38 A1
Ras Budran 18 B3
Ras Samadai 29 H5
Rod Kharuf 34 D3
Sabkhet el Bardawil 14 B2
Sharm an-Naga 25 E4
Sharm el Bahari 29 F2
Sharm el-Sheikh 25 F1
Strait of Tiran 19 F6
Suez Canal (Qana el Suweis) 13 G3
Trat el Mansuriya 13 E3
Wadi 'Abbad 28 C5
Wadi Abu Aggag 33 H3
Wadi Abu Alawi 13 F6
Wadi Abu Aqieri 24 D4
Wadi Abu Domi 33 G2
Wadi Abu Durma 13 F6
Wadi Abu el Gain 18 C2
Wadi Abu Ghurra 33 F1
Wadi Abu Ghusun 35 F1
Wadi Abu Gidil 14 C5
Wadi Abu Had 24 C2
Wadi Abu Had 34 D6, 38 D1
Wadi Abu 'Igeidi 28 D4
Wadi Abu Kharaga 17 F5
Wadi Abu Ligan 13 H2
Wadi Abu Markha 33 F2
Wadi Abu Marwa 24 C3
Wadi Abu Nafukh 23 H6
Wadi Abu Rimth 17 F4
Wadi Abu Risha 17 F3
Wadi Abu Salan 27 H6
Wadi Abu Shih 23 G5
Wadi Abu Shihat 24 C6
Wadi Abu Tareifia 23 G5
Wadi Abu Tareifya 18 D1
Wadi Abu Thadib 28 C2
Wadi Abu Ziran 29 E2
Wadi Allaqi 39 E3
Wadi 'Antar 34 D1
Wadi 'Araba 17 G3
Wadi 'Asal 29 F2

Wadi Akhdar 18 D4
Wadi al-Aat 25 F1
Wadi al Araban (J) 15 H4
Wadi al-Battikh 26 A-B3
Wadi al Dabr (SA) 19 G3
Wadi al Hasa (J) 15 H2
Wadi al Hasha (SA) 19 G3
Wadi al-Mahla 19 F3
Wadi al Maqnah (SA) 19 G5
Wadi Arhab 17 E4
Wadi Askhar 17 G3
Wadi Atfih 17 E2
Wadi Bad' 17 G1
Wadi Bali' 24 D3
Wadi Barud 24 D5
Wadi Beizah 28 D6, 29 E5
Wadi Bir el Ain 23 G5
Wadi Dahasa 23 E2
Wadi Dara 18 C6
Wadi Dib 24 C1
Wadi Difeit 38 C3
Wadi Digla 15 H3
Wadi Dubur 29 G4
Wadi el 'Abeid 17 G4
Wadi el Abyad 17 G2
Wadi el Agheidara 14 C5
Wadi el 'Allaqi 38 A1
Wadi el Arak 29 E3
Wadi el Arish 14 D3-5, 15 E4, 18 C1
Wadi el 'Ashara 15 H3
Wadi el Asyuti 23 E4-G3
Wadi el Atedni 28 C1
Wadi el Atrash 24 C4
Wadi el Bahei 15 E5
Wadi el Barramiya 28 D5
Wadi el Batur 28 D4
Wadi el Beida 15 F6
Wadi el Biyar 19 E3
Wadi el Bruk 14 D5
Wadi el Bustan 16 D6
Wadi el Butum 19 F2
Wadi el Dakhal 18 A4
Wadi el Deir 18 A4
Wadi el Fahdi 15 E5
Wadi el Fatira el Zarga 24 C5
Wadi el Furn 13 F6
Wadi el Gafra 13 F5
Wadi el Garf 18 D3
Wadi el Ghabiya 18 D1
Wadi el Ghuz 24 C4
Wadi el Gidami 24 C6
Wadi el Giddi 14 A5
Wadi el Gimmeiza 33 F2
Wadi el Gurur 15 E4
Wadi el Hadira 14 C5
Wadi el Hagg 14 A5
Wadi el Hamar 15 E5
Wadi el Hamma 14 C3
Wadi el Heisi 19 F2
Wadi el Higayib 14 B4
Wadi el-Homur 18 C3
Wadi el Imrani 23 E3
Wadi el Kamak 27 G2
Wadi el Kharit 33 H1,34 B2, 35 E2
Wadi el Khiwa 35 F3
Wadi el Ellawi 33 H2,34 A2
Wadi el Madamud 28 B3
Wadi el Mahamid 27 H4
Wadi el Markh 24 C6
Wadi el Mathula 28 B2
Wadi el Mileiz 14 C5
Wadi el Mishash 28 C3
Wadi el Miyah 28 D5
Wadi el Miyah 29 F3
Wadi el Muweih el 'Atshan 28 C1
Wadi el Natila 14 C5
Wadi el Natrun 12 B5
Wadi el Nihiya 17 E4

Wadi el Nu'umiya 17 E2
Wadi el Qash 28 D2
Wadi el Qobbaniya 33 G2
Wadi el Qreiya 24 B6
Wadi el-Quffa 34 B4
Wadi el Radda 28 A5
Wadi el Rana 14 A6
Wadi el Rimth 13 F5
Wadi el Ruaq 19 E1
Wadi el Saheira 14 C6
Wadi el Saheira 18 B1
Wadi el Saqi 24 D6
Wadi el Shaghab 28 C4-5
Wadi el Shaki 28 B4
Wadi el Sheik 16 D5
Wadi el Sheikh 18 D4
Wadi el Shuna 17 G1
Wadi el Sihrig 37 F3
Wadi el Siq 18 B2
Wadi el Sirag 28 C6
Wadi el Surai 28 B2
Wadi el Tarfa 16 D6, 17 E6, 17 H5
Wadi el Ushra 33 F1
Wadi el Watan 13 F4
Wadi el Wirag 17 E2
Wadi Faliq el Sahl 24 D4
Wadi Faqira 16 D4
Wadi Fatira 24 B5
Wadi Feiran 18 C4
Wadi Gabgaba 38 A2
Wadi Garara 34 C3
Wadi Garawi 13 E6
Wadi Garf 29 F5
Wadi Gemal 29 H6
Wadi Gha'ib 19 F4
Wadi Ghadir 29 H5
Wadi Gharandal 18 B2
Wadi Gharba 17 F1
Wadi Gharib 18 B6
Wadi Gheuta 18 C1
Wadi Ghuweibba 17 G1
Wadi Gira 19 E2
Wadi Gurdi 24 A5
Wadi Habib 23 F3-G4
Wadi Hafya 29 F5
Wadi Hagul 13 G6
Wadi Haimur 38 B2
Wadi Hamama 24 C6
Wadi Hamamid 35 E2
Wadi Hamid 37 E3
Wadi Hammad 24 B5
Wadi Hareidin 15 E2
Wadi Hasana 14 D4
Wadi Hawashiya 17 H6
Wadi Hayira 17 E1
Wadi Hellal 28 B5
Wadi Hideidun 18 C1
Wadi Hodein 35 F5
Wadi Hof 13 E6
Wadi Hommath 13 H6
Wadi Huluz 35 E2
Wadi Humi 19 E5
Wadi 'Ibada 22 D2
Wadi 'Irkas 17 G4
Wadi 'Iseili 13 F6
Wadi Ifal (SA) 19 H5
Wadi Ilhami 28 A5
Wadi Imlaha 18 D6
Wadi Imu 23 E4
Wadi Kahaliya 13 G6
Wadi Kalabsha 33 F5
Wadi Kareim 29 E2
Wadi Khadakhid 15 F5
Wadi Khashab 34 C2
Wadi Kheibar 28 A5
Wadi Khoreiza 15 E5
Wadi Khuda 35 G4
Wadi Khuzam 28 B3

Wadi Kid 19 F6
Wadi Kurkur 33 F3
Wadi Kurusku 37 G3
Wadi Lahata 18 A1
Wadi Lahemi 35 G2
Wadi Lig 19 F5
Wadi Lishyab 17 E3
Wadi Ma'sar 29 E3
Wadi Mahariq 23 G2
Wadi Mahash 19 E6
Wadi Malha 17 H3
Wadi Malhaq 19 F5
Wadi Manih 28 D3
Wadi Mattala 18 B3
Wadi Midrik 28 D6
Wadi Milaha 24 C2
Wadi Mir 18 D5
Wadi Muathil 17 E4
Wadi Mubarak 29 F4
Wadi Murra 38 C2
Wadi Musa (J) 15 H4
Wadi Muweilha 29 E6
Wadi Muweilih 16 C4
Wadi Muftan 13 F5
Wadi Naq'el Teir 24 B6
Wadi Nasb 19 E5
Wadi Natash 29 F6
Wadi Natash 34 B2
Wadi No'oz 17 G2
Wadi Nugrus 29 H6
Wadi Oko (S) 40 B4
Wadi Or 37 E3
Wadi Qasab 23 G6-H5
Wadi Qena 17 G2
Wadi Qena 24 A2
Wadi Qena 24 B6
Wadi Qideira 19 E2
Wadi Qiraiya 15 E4-5
Wadi Quei 25 E6
Wadi Quss 17 E4
Wadi Rahaba 35 G5
Wadi Raiaitit 34 D4
Wadi Rimidin 27 H6
Wadi Rishrash 17 F2
Wadi Rod Ayid 28 C2
Wadi Saal 19 E4
Wadi Safaga 25 E5
Wadi Sannur 17 F3
Wadi Sanur 17 E4
Wadi Seiga 38 C2
Wadi Seih 18 D3
Wadi Serimtai 40 C3
Wadi Sha'it 28 D6,29 F6
Wadi Sharuna 16 D5
Wadi Sheitun 23 H5
Wadi Shilman 38 B2
Wadi Sidri 18 C4
Wadi Sillim 28 C6
Wasi Sku 33 H6
Wadi Somar 18 B1
Wadi Sudr 18 B1
Wadi Tag el Wabar 23 F6
Wadi Taiyiba 19 E2
Wadi Thiman 18 D6
Wadi Tunsah 34 D4
Wadi Tushka 37 E2
Wadi Umm 'Araka 23 H6
Wadi Umm 'Omeiyid 23 H2, 24 A2
Wadi Umm 'Udi 33 H2
Wadi Umm Adawi 19 E6
Wadi Umm Aria 17 H5
Wadi Umm Balad 24 A2
Wadi Umm Dawita 38 B3
Wadi Umm Dorni 38 B3
Wadi Umm Diheis 24 D3
Wadi Umm Garfein (SA) 19 G2
Wadi Umm Gheig 29 G3
Wadi Umm Had 28 D2

PLANET TALK

Lonely Planet's FREE quarterly newsletter

We love hearing from you and think you'd like to hear from us.

When...is the right time to see reindeer in Finland?
Where...can you hear the best palm-wine music in Ghana?
How...do you get from Asunción to Areguá by steam train?
What...is the best way to see India?

For the answer to these and many other questions read PLANET TALK.

Every issue is packed with up-to-date travel news and advice including:

- a letter from Lonely Planet co-founders Tony and Maureen Wheeler
- go behind the scenes on the road with a Lonely Planet author
- feature article on an important and topical travel issue
- a selection of recent letters from travellers
- details on forthcoming Lonely Planet promotions
- complete list of Lonely Planet products

To join our mailing list contact any Lonely Planet office.

Also available: Lonely Planet T-shirts. 100% heavyweight cotton.

LONELY PLANET ONLINE

Get the latest travel information before you leave or while you're on the road

Whether you've just begun planning your next trip, or you're chasing down specific info on currency regulations or visa requirements, check out the Lonely Planet World Wide Web site for up-to-the-minute travel information.

As well as travel profiles of your favourite destinations (including interactive maps and full-colour photos), you'll find current reports from our army of researchers and other travellers, updates on health and visas, travel advisories, and the ecological and political issues you need to be aware of as you travel.

There's an online travellers' forum (the Thorn Tree) where you can share your experiences of life on the road, meet travel companions and ask other travellers for their recommendations and advice. We also have plenty of links to other Web sites useful to independent travellers.

With tens of thousands of visitors a month, the Lonely Planet Web site is one of the most popular on the Internet and has won a number of awards including GNN's Best of the Net travel award.

http://www.lonelyplanet.com

LONELY PLANET GUIDES TO AFRICA

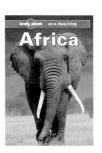

Africa on a shoestring
From Marrakesh to Kampala, Mozambique to Mauritania, Johannesburg to Cairo – this guidebook has all the facts on travelling in Africa. Comprehensive information on more than 50 countries.

Arabic (Egyptian) phrasebook
This handy phrasebook is packed with words and phrases to cover almost every situation. Arabic script is included making this phrasebook useful to travellers in most other Arabic-speaking countries.

Arabic (Moroccan) phrasebook
Whether finding a hotel or asking for a meal, this indispensable phrasebook will help travellers to North Africa make their travels with ease. This phrasebook also includes Arabic script and a helpful pronunciation guide.

Cape Town city guide
Cape Town offers lively cafés, magnificent surf beaches and superb mountain walks. This indispensable guide is packed with insider tips for both business and leisure travellers.

Central Africa
This guide tells where to go to meet gorillas in the jungle, how to catch a steamer down the Congo...even the best beer to wash down grilled boa constrictor! Covers Cameroun, the Central African Republic, Chad, the Congo, Equatorial Guinea, Gabon, São Tomé & Principe, and Zaïre.

East Africa
Detailed information on Kenya, Uganda, Rwanda, Burundi, eastern Zaïre and Tanzania. The latest edition includes a 32-page full-colour Safari Guide.

Egypt
This guide takes you into and beyond the spectacular and mysterious pyramids, temples, tombs, monasteries, mosques and bustling main streets of Egypt.

Ethiopian (Amharic) phrasebook
You'll enjoy Ethiopia a whole lot more if you can speak some of the language. All the phrases you need are at your fingertips in this handy phrasebook.

Kenya
This superb guide features a 32-page Safari Guide with colour photographs, illustrations and information on East Africa's famous wildlife.

Morocco
This thoroughly revised and expanded guide is full of down-to-earth information and reliable advice for every budget. It includes a 20-page colour section on Moroccan arts and crafts and information on trekking routes in the High Atlas and Rif Mountains.

North Africa
A most detailed and comprehensive guide to the Maghreb – Morocco, Algeria, Tunisia and Libya. It points the way to fascinating bazaars, superb beaches and the vast Sahara, and is packed with reliable advice for every budget. This new guide includes a 20-page full colour section on Moroccan arts and crafts.

South Africa, Lesotho & Swaziland
Travel to southern Africa and you'll be surprised by its cultural diversity and incredible beauty. There's no better place to see Africa's amazing wildlife. All the essential travel details are included in this guide as well as information about wildlife reserves, and a 32-page full colour Safari Guide.

Swahili phrasebook
Swahili is a major lingua franca of the African continent. This handy phrasebook will prove invaluable for travellers to Africa.

Trekking in East Africa
Practical, first-hand information for trekkers for a region renowned for its spectacular national parks and rewarding trekking trails. Covers treks in Kenya, Tanzania, Uganda and Malawi.

West Africa
All the necessary information for independent travel in Benin, Burkino Faso, Cape Verde, Côte d'Ivoire, The Gambia, Ghana, Guinea, Guinea-Bissau, Liberia, Mali, Mauritania, Niger, Nigeria, Senegal, Sierra Leone and Togo. Includes a colour section on local culture and birdlife.

Zimbabwe, Botswana & Namibia
Exotic wildlife, breathtaking scenery and fascinating people...this comprehensive guide shows a wilder, older side of Africa for the adventurous traveller. Includes a 32-page colour Safari Guide.

Zimbabwe, Botswana & Namibia travel atlas
Make your journey to this spectacular region with the handiest, most accurate maps available.

LONELY PLANET GUIDES TO THE MIDDLE EAST

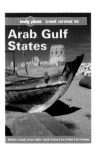

Arab Gulf States
This comprehensive, practical guide to travel in the Arab Gulf States covers travel in Bahrain, Kuwait, Oman, Qatar, Saudi Arabia and the United Arab Emirates. A concise history and language section is included for each country.

Iran
As well as practical travel details, the author provides background information that will fascinate adventurers and armchair travellers alike.

Israel & the Palestinian Territories
Journey back thousands of years exploring the sites that have inspired the world's major regions; float on the Dead Sea; go camel trekking in the Negev; volunteer for a unique kibbutz experience; and explore the holy city of Jerusalem and cosmopolitan Tel Aviv. This guide is packed with insight and practical information for all budgets.

Jordan & Syria
Two countries with a wealth of natural and historical attractions for the adventurous travellers...12th century Crusader castles, ruined cities and haunting desert landscapes.

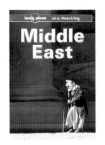

Middle East on a shoestring
All the travel advice and essential information for travel in Afghanistan, Bahrain, Egypt, Iran, Iraq, Israel, Jordan, Kuwait, Lebanon, Oman, Qatar, Saudi Arabia, Syria, Turkey, United Arab Emirates and Yemen.

Trekking in Turkey
Explore beyond Turkey's coastline and you will be surprised to discover that Turkey has mountains to rival those found in Nepal.

Turkey
Experience Turkey with this highly-acclaimed, best selling guide. Packed with information for the traveller on any budget, it's your essential companion.

Turkish phrasebook
Practical words and phrases and a handy pronunciation guide, make this phrasebook essential for travellers visiting Turkey.

Yemen
Discover the timeless history and intrigue of the land of the *Arabian Nights* with the most comprehensive guide to Yemen.

Also available:

The Gates of Damascus by Lieve Joris (translated by Sam Garrett)
This best-selling book is a beautifully drawn portrait of day-to-day life in modern Syria. Through her intimate contact with local people, Lieve Joris draws us into the fascinating world that lies behind the gates of Damascus.

LONELY PLANET PRODUCTS

AFRICA
Africa on a shoestring • Arabic (Moroccan) phrasebook • Cape Town city guide • Central Africa • East Africa • Egypt • Egypt travel atlas • Ethiopian (Amharic) phrasebook • Kenya • Morocco • North Africa • South Africa, Lesotho & Swaziland • Swahili phrasebook • Trekking in East Africa• West Africa • Zimbabwe, Botswana & Namibia • Zimbabwe, Botswana & Namibia travel atlas

ANTARCTICA
Antarctica

AUSTRALIA & THE PACIFIC
Australia • Australian phrasebook • Bushwalking in Australia • Bushwalking in Papua New Guinea • Fiji • Fijian phrasebook • Islands of Australia's Great Barrier Reef • Melbourne city guide • Micronesia • New Caledonia • New South Wales & the ACT • New Zealand • Northern Territory • Outback Australia • Papua New Guinea • Papua New Guinea phrasebook • Queensland • Rarotonga & the Cook Islands • Samoa • Solomon Islands • South Australia • Sydney city guide • Tahiti & French Polynesia • Tasmania • Tonga • Tramping in New Zealand • Vanuatu • Victoria • Western Australia
Travel Literature: Islands in the Clouds • Sean & David's Long Drive

CENTRAL AMERICA & THE CARIBBEAN
Central America on a shoestring • Costa Rica • Eastern Caribbean • Guatemala, Belize & Yucatán: La Ruta Maya • Jamaica

EUROPE
Austria • Baltic States & Kaliningrad • Baltics States phrasebook • Britain • Central Europe on a shoestring • Central Europe phrasebook • Czech & Slovak Republics • Denmark • Dublin city guide • Eastern Europe on a shoestring • Eastern Europe phrasebook • Finland • France • Greece • Greek phrasebook • Hungary • Iceland, Greenland & the Faroe Islands • Ireland • Italy • Mediterranean Europe on a shoestring • Mediterranean Europe phrasebook • Paris city guide • Poland • Prague city guide • Russia, Ukraine & Belarus • Russian phrasebook • Scandinavian & Baltic Europe on a shoestring • Scandinavian Europe phrasebook • Slovenia • St Petersburg city guide • Switzerland • Trekking in Greece • Trekking in Spain • Ukrainian phrasebook • Vienna city guide • Walking in Switzerland • Western Europe on a shoestring • Western Europe phrasebook

INDIAN SUBCONTINENT
Bangladesh • Bengali phrasebook • Delhi city guide • Hindi/Urdu phrasebook • India • India & Bangladesh travel atlas • Indian Himalaya • Karakoram Highway • Nepal • Nepali phrasebook • Pakistan • Sri Lanka • Sri Lanka phrasebook • Trekking in the Indian Himalaya • Trekking in the Nepal Himalaya
Travel Literature: Shopping for Buddhas

ISLANDS OF THE INDIAN OCEAN
Madagascar & Comoros • Maldives & Islands of the East Indian Ocean • Mauritius, Réunion & Seychelles

MIDDLE EAST & CENTRAL ASIA
Arab Gulf States • Arabic (Egyptian) phrasebook • Central Asia • Iran • Israel & the Palestinian Territories • Israel & the Palestinian Territories travel atlas • Jordan & Syria • Jordan, Syria & Lebanon travel atlas • Middle East • Turkey • Turkish phrasebook • Trekking in Turkey • Yemen
Travel Literature: The Gates of Damascus

NORTH AMERICA
Alaska • Backpacking in Alaska • Baja California • California & Nevada • Canada • Hawaii • Honolulu city guide • Los Angeles city guide • Mexico • Miami city guide • New England • Pacific Northwest USA • Rocky Mountain States • San Francisco city guide • Southwest USA • USA phrasebook

NORTH-EAST ASIA
Beijing city guide • Cantonese phrasebook • China • Hong Kong city guide • Hong Kong, Macau & Canton • Japan • Japanese phrasebook • Japanese audio pack • Korea • Korean phrasebook • Mandarin phrasebook • Mongolia • Mongolian phrasebook • North-East Asia on a shoestring • Seoul city guide • Taiwan • Tibet • Tibet phrasebook • Tokyo city guide
Travel Literature: Lost Japan

SOUTH AMERICA
Argentina, Uruguay & Paraguay • Bolivia • Brazil • Brazilian phrasebook • Buenos Aires city guide • Chile & Easter Island • Chile travel atlas • Colombia • Ecuador & the Galápagos Islands • Latin American Spanish phrasebook • Peru • Quechua phrasebook • Rio de Janeiro city guide • South America on a shoestring • Trekking in the Patagonian Andes • Venezuela
Travel Literature: Full Circle: A South American Journey

SOUTH-EAST ASIA
Bali & Lombok • Bangkok city guide • Burmese phrasebook• Cambodia • Ho Chi Minh city guide • Indonesia • Indonesian phrasebook • Indonesian audio pack • Jakarta city guide • Java • Laos • Laos travel atlas • Lao phrasebook • Malaysia, Singapore & Brunei • Myanmar (Burma) • Philippines • Pilipino phrasebook • Singapore city guide • South-East Asia on a shoestring • Thailand • Thailand travel atlas • Thai phrasebook • Thai Hill Tribes phrasebook • Thai audio pack • Vietnam • Vietnamese phrasebook • Vietnam travel atlas

LONELY PLANET TRAVEL ATLASES

Conventional fold-out maps work just fine when you're planning your trip on the kitchen table, but have you ever tried to use one – or the half-dozen you sometimes need to cover a country – while you're actually on the road? Even if you have the origami skills necessary to unfold the sucker, you know that flimsy bit of paper is not going to last the distance.

"Lonely Planet travel atlases are designed to make it through your journey in one piece – the sturdy book format is based on the assumption that since all travellers want to make it home without punctures, tears or wrinkles, the maps they use should too."

The travel atlases contain detailed, colour maps that are checked on the road by our travel authors to ensure their accuracy. Place name spellings are consistent with our associated guidebooks, so you can use the atlas and the guidebook hand in hand as you travel and find what you are looking for. Unlike conventional maps, each atlas has a comprehensive index, as well as a detailed legend and helpful 'getting around' sections translated into five languages. Sorry, no free steak knives...

Features of this series include:

- full-colour maps, plus colour photos
- maps researched and checked by Lonely Planet authors
- place names correspond with Lonely Planet guidebooks, so there are no confusing spelling differences
- complete index of features and place names
- atlas legend and travelling information presented in five languages: English, French, German, Spanish and Japanese

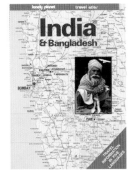

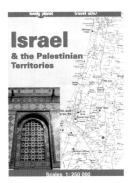

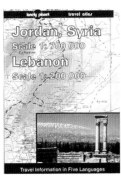

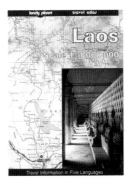

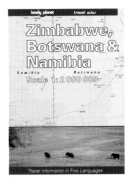

THE LONELY PLANET STORY

Lonely Planet published its first book in 1973 in response to the numerous 'How did you do it?' questions Maureen and Tony Wheeler were asked after driving, bussing, hitching, sailing and railing their way from England to Australia.

Written at a kitchen table and hand collated, trimmed and stapled, *Across Asia on the Cheap* became an instant local bestseller, inspiring thoughts of another book.

Eighteen months in South-East Asia resulted in their second guide, *South-East Asia on a shoestring*, which they put together in a backstreet Chinese hotel in Singapore in 1975. The 'yellow bible', as it quickly became known to backpackers around the world, soon became *the* guide to the region. It has sold well over half a million copies and is now in its 8th edition, still retaining its familiar yellow cover.

Today there are over 180 titles, including travel guides, walking guides, language kits & phrasebooks, travel atlases and travel literature. The company is one of the largest travel publishers in the world. Although Lonely Planet initially specialised in guides to Asia, we now cover most regions of the world, including the Pacific, North America, South America, Africa, the Middle East and Europe.

The emphasis continues to be on travel for independent travellers. Tony and Maureen still travel for several months of each year and play an active part in the writing, updating and quality control of Lonely Planet's guides.

They have been joined by over 70 authors and 170 staff at our offices in Melbourne (Australia), Oakland (USA), London (UK) and Paris (France). Travellers themselves also make a valuable contribution to the guides through the feedback we receive in thousands of letters each year.

The people at Lonely Planet strongly believe that travellers can make a positive contribution to the countries they visit, both through their appreciation of the countries' culture, wildlife and natural features, and through the money they spend. In addition, the company makes a direct contribution to the countries and regions it covers. Since 1986 a percentage of the income from each book has been donated to ventures such as famine relief in Africa; aid projects in India; agricultural projects in Central America; Greenpeace's efforts to halt French nuclear testing in the Pacific; and Amnesty International.

'I hope we send people out with the right attitude about travel. You realise when you travel that there are so many different perspectives about the world, so we hope these books will make people more interested in what they see.'

– Tony Wheeler

LONELY PLANET PUBLICATIONS

AUSTRALIA (HEAD OFFICE)
PO Box 617, Hawthorn 3122, Victoria
tel: (03) 9819 1877   fax: (03) 9819 6459
e-mail: talk2us@lonelyplanet.com.au

UK
10 Barley Mow Passage,
Chiswick, London W4 4PH
tel: (0181) 742 3161 fax: (0181) 742 2772
e-mail: 100413.3551@compuserve.com

USA
Embarcadero West,155 Filbert St, Suite 251,
Oakland, CA 94607
tel: (510) 893 8555   TOLL FREE: 800 275-8555
fax: (510) 893 8563
e-mail: info@lonelyplanet.com

FRANCE
71 bis rue du Cardinal Lemoine, 75005 Paris
tel: 1 44 32 06 20   fax: 1 46 34 72 55
e-mail: 100560.415@compuserve.com

World Wide Web: http://www.lonelyplanet.com/

EGYPT TRAVEL ATLAS

Dear Traveller,

We would appreciate it if you would take the time to write your thoughts on this page and return it to a Lonely Planet office.
Only with your help can we continue to make sure this atlas is as accurate and travel-friendly as possible.

Where did you acquire this atlas?

Bookstore ☐   In which section of the store did you find it, i.e. maps or travel guidebooks? ....

Map shop ☐   Direct mail ☐   Other ....

How are you using this travel atlas?

On the road ☐   For home reference ☐   For business reference ☐

Other ....

When travelling with this atlas, did you find any inaccuracies?

....

....

How does the atlas fare on the road in terms of ease of use and durability?

....

Are you using the atlas in conjunction with an LP guidebook/s?   Yes ☐   No ☐

Which one/s?...

Have you bought any other LP products for your trip?...

Do you think the information on the travel atlas maps is presented clearly?   Yes ☐   No ☐

If English is not your main language, do you find the language sections useful?   Yes ☐   No ☐

Please list any features you think should be added to the travel atlas.

....

....

....

Would you consider purchasing another atlas in this series?   Yes ☐   No ☐

Please indicate your age group.

15-25 ☐   26-35 ☐   36-45 ☐   46-55 ☐   56-65 ☐   66+ ☐

Do you have any other general comments you'd like to make?

....

....

....

....

P.S. Thank you very much for this information. The best contributions will be rewarded with a free copy of a Lonely Planet book.
We give away lots of books, but, unfortunately, not every contributor receives one.

Notes

Notes